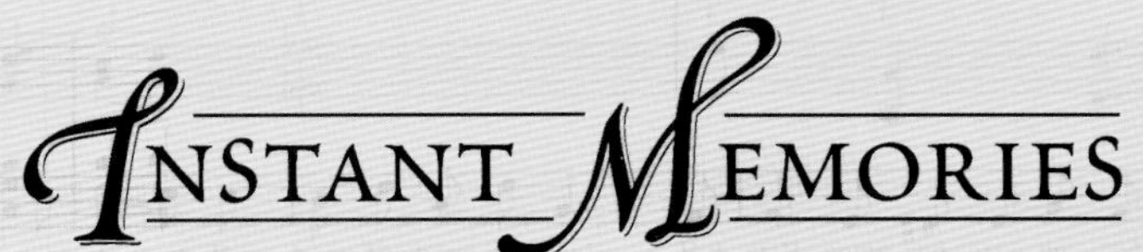

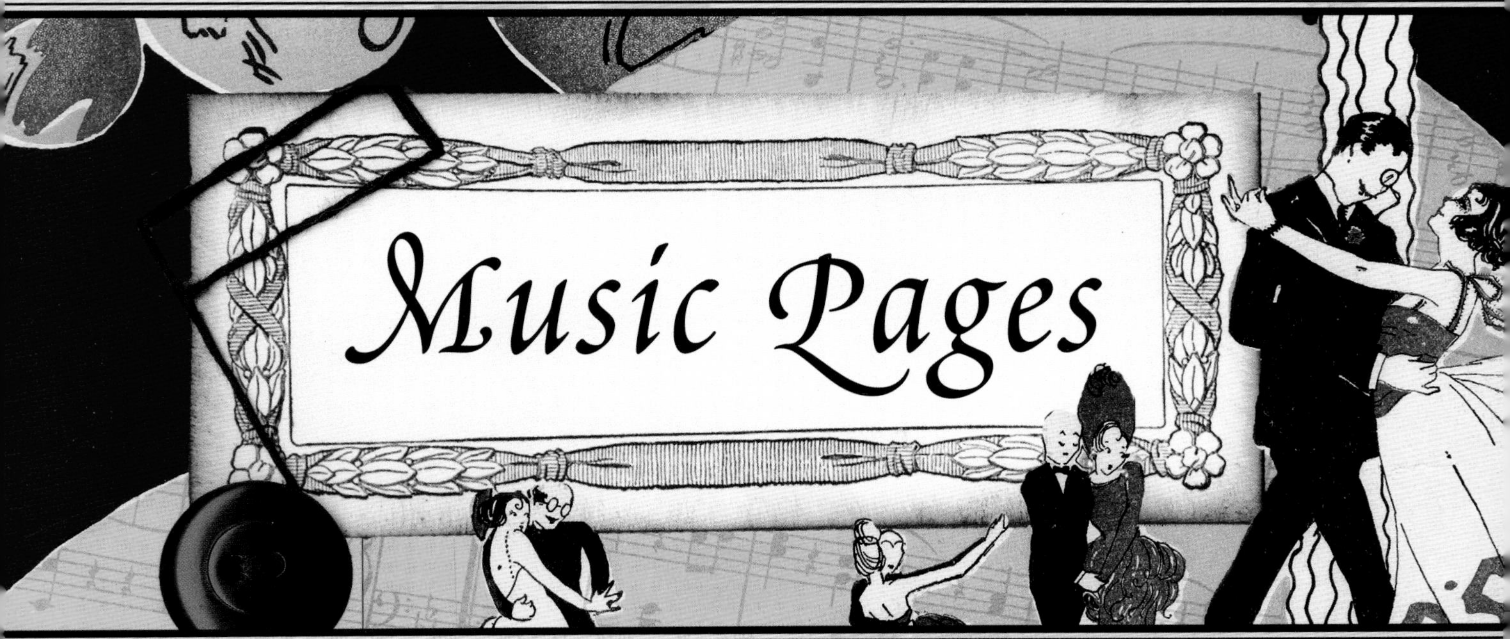

Music Pages

Ready-to-Use Scrapbook Pages

Andrea Vetten-Marley

A LARK/CHAPELLE BOOK
A Division of Sterling Publishing Co., Inc.
New York

A Lark/Chapelle Book

Chapelle, Ltd., Inc.
P.O. Box 9255, Ogden, UT 84409
(801) 621-2777 • (801) 621-2788 Fax
e-mail: chapelle@chapelleltd.com
Web site: www.chapelleltd.com

10 9 8 7 6 5 4 3 2 1

First Edition

Published by Lark Books, A Division of
Sterling Publishing Co., Inc.
387 Park Avenue South, New York, N.Y. 10016

Distributed in Canada by Sterling Publishing,
c/o Canadian Manda Group, 165 Dufferin Street
Toronto, Ontario, Canada M6K 3H6

Distributed in the United Kingdom by GMC Distribution Services,
Castle Place, 166 High Street, Lewes, East Sussex, England BN7 1XU

Distributed in Australia by Capricorn Link (Australia) Pty Ltd.,
P.O. Box 704, Windsor, NSW 2756 Australia

Manufactured in China

ISBN 13: 978-1-57990-991-8
ISBN 10: 1-57990-991-4

For information about custom editions, special sales, premium and corporate purchases, please contact Sterling Special Sales Department at 800-805-5489 or specialsales@sterlingpub.com.

Introduction

Scrapbooking is a wonderful way to document special day-to-day events, holidays, celebrations, and family history. However, not everyone has the time or the money to do what it takes to create show-stopping scrapbook pages. That's where the *Instant Memories Ready-to-Use Scrapbook Pages* series comes in. The top designers in the field have done all the work for you—simply add your favorite photos to their layouts and you're done! Or add a few embellishments, such as a charm or ribbon, and you have a unique personalized page in minutes. You can tear the pages directly from the book, photocopy them to use time and again, or print them from the enclosed CD.

As an added bonus in the *Instant Memories* series, we have included hundreds of rare, vintage images on the enclosed CD-Rom. From Victorian postcards to hand-painted beautiful borders and frames, it would take years to acquire a collection like this. However, with this easy-to-use resource, you'll have them all right here, right now, to use for any computer project over and again. Each image has been reproduced to the highest quality standard for photocopying and scanning and can be reduced or enlarged to suit your needs.

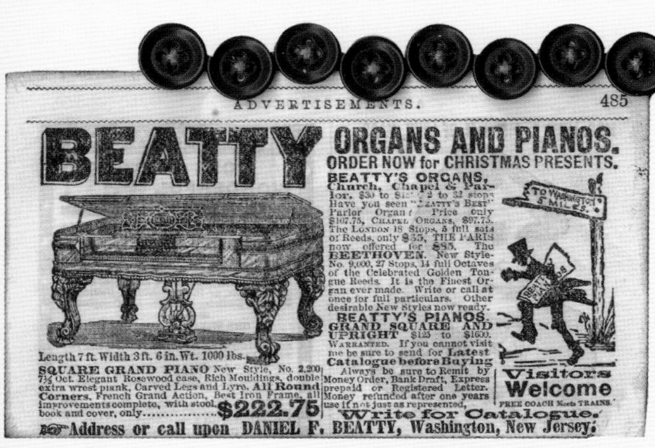

Perfect for paper crafting, scrapbooking, and fabric transfers, *Instant Memories* books will inspire you to explore new avenues of creativity. We've included a sampling of ideas to get you started, but the best part is using your imagination to create your own projects. Be sure to look for other books in this series as we continue to search the markets for wonderful vintage images.

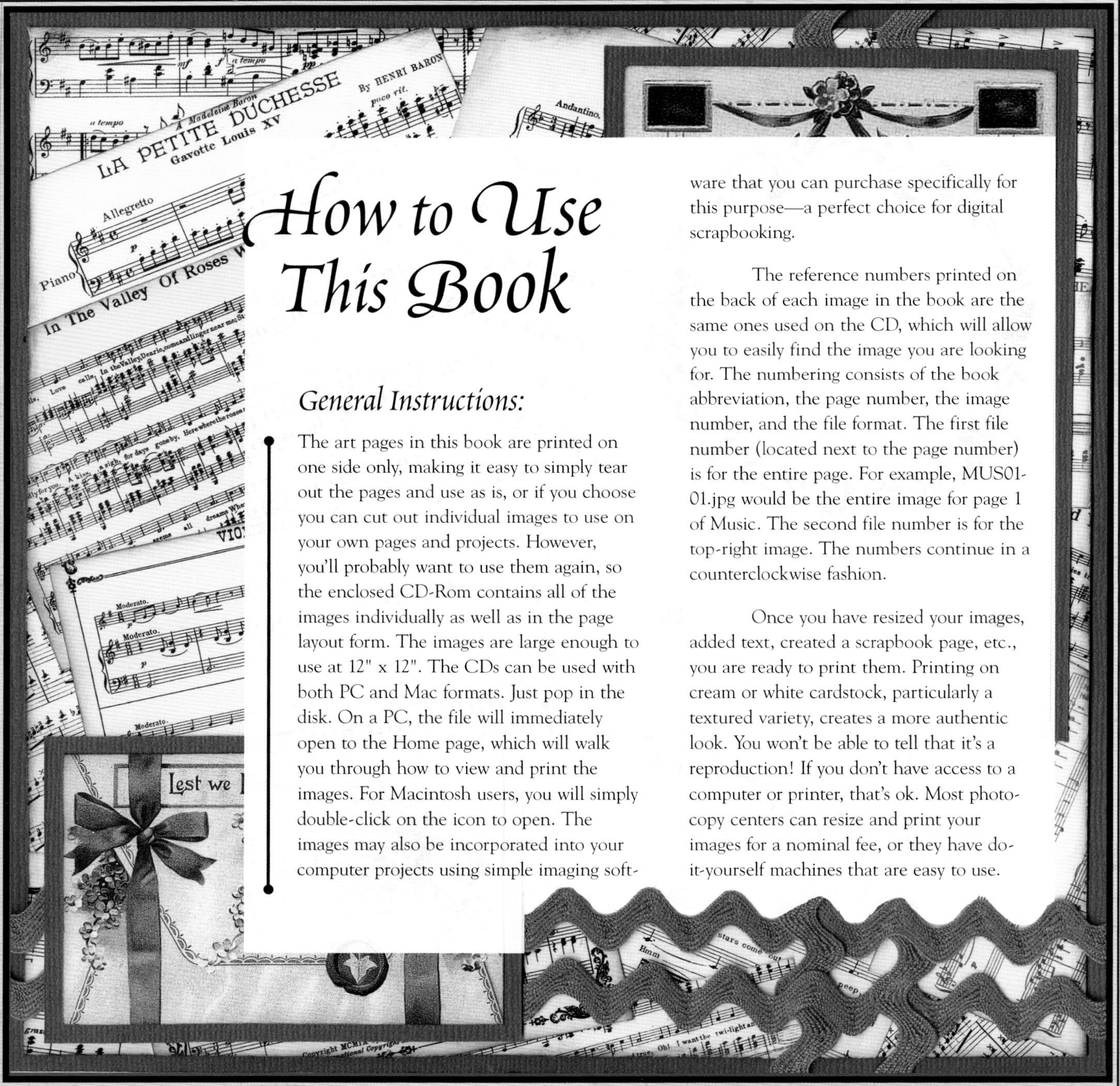

How to Use This Book

General Instructions:

The art pages in this book are printed on one side only, making it easy to simply tear out the pages and use as is, or if you choose you can cut out individual images to use on your own pages and projects. However, you'll probably want to use them again, so the enclosed CD-Rom contains all of the images individually as well as in the page layout form. The images are large enough to use at 12" x 12". The CDs can be used with both PC and Mac formats. Just pop in the disk. On a PC, the file will immediately open to the Home page, which will walk you through how to view and print the images. For Macintosh users, you will simply double-click on the icon to open. The images may also be incorporated into your computer projects using simple imaging software that you can purchase specifically for this purpose—a perfect choice for digital scrapbooking.

The reference numbers printed on the back of each image in the book are the same ones used on the CD, which will allow you to easily find the image you are looking for. The numbering consists of the book abbreviation, the page number, the image number, and the file format. The first file number (located next to the page number) is for the entire page. For example, MUS01-01.jpg would be the entire image for page 1 of Music. The second file number is for the top-right image. The numbers continue in a counterclockwise fashion.

Once you have resized your images, added text, created a scrapbook page, etc., you are ready to print them. Printing on cream or white cardstock, particularly a textured variety, creates a more authentic look. You won't be able to tell that it's a reproduction! If you don't have access to a computer or printer, that's ok. Most photocopy centers can resize and print your images for a nominal fee, or they have do-it-yourself machines that are easy to use.

Ideas for Using the Images:

Scrapbooking: These images are perfect for both heritage and modern scrapbook pages. Simply use the image as a frame, accent piece, or border. For those of you with limited time, the page layouts in this book have been created so that you can use them as they are. Simply print out or photocopy the desired page, attach a photograph into one of the boxes, add your own journaling, and you have a beautiful designer scrapbook page in minutes. Be sure to print your images onto acid-free cardstock so the pages will last a lifetime.

Cards: Some computer programs allow images to be inserted into a card template, simplifying cardmaking. If this is not an option, simply use the images as accent pieces on the front or inside of the card. Use a bone folder to score the card's fold to create a more professional look.

Decoupage/Collage Projects: For decoupage or collage projects, photocopy or print the image onto a thinner paper such as copier paper. Thin paper adheres to projects more effectively. Decoupage medium glues and seals the project, creating a gloss or matte finish when dry, thus protecting the image. Vintage images are beautiful when decoupaged to cigar boxes, glass plates, and even wooden plaques. The possibilities are endless.

Fabric Arts: Vintage images can be used in just about any fabric craft imaginable: wall hangings, quilts, bags, or baby bibs. Either transfer the image onto the fabric by using a special iron-on paper, or by printing the image directly onto the fabric, using a temporary iron-on stabilizer that stabilizes the fabric to feed through a printer. These items are available at most craft and sewing stores. If the item will be washed, it is better to print directly on the fabric. For either method, follow the instructions on the package.

Wood Transfers: It is now possible to print images on wood. Use this exciting technique to create vintage plaques, clocks, frames, and more. A simple, inexpensive transfer tool is available at most large craft or home improvement stores, or online from various manufacturers. You simply place the photocopy of the image you want, face down, onto the surface and use the tool to transfer the image onto the wood. This process requires a copy from a laser printer, which means you will probably have to get your copies made at a copy center. Refer to manufacturer's instructions for additional details. There are other transfer products available that can be used with wood. Choose the one that is easiest for you.

Gallery of Ideas

These music images can be used in a variety of projects: cards, scrapbook pages, and decoupage projects to name a few. The images can be used as they are shown in the layout, or you can copy and clip out individual images, or even portions or multitudes of images. The following pages contain a collection of ideas to inspire you to use your imagination and create one-of-a-kind treasures.

Idea 1

An Altered Art CD Card is fun to make and to give. Take two CD's and glue images to both sides of each CD. Make certain to cut out the CD center. Add words to create your message using rub-on alphabets, game pieces, or a label maker. Punch 3 holes on the left side of both CDs. Thread ribbon through and tie.

Idea 2

Take your little star and let her shine bright atop a background of sheet music. Add a name and date to remember.

art page 40

Idea 3

Simply add a favorite picture of someone special to finish this page.

art page 36

Idea 4

Add your favorite "series" photographs and then lightly color your page with colored pencils to highlight the colors in the photographs.

art page 5

Idea 5

Create a vintage girlfriend page by overlaying your image on top of the music collage and then embellishing with ribbons, ric rac, buttons, and lace.

art page 16

art page 13

Idea 6

Add your favorite winter snow pictures to help this page come to life. The buttons look like little snowflakes.

Idea 7

Make this Mother's Day Scrapbook cover by adhering one of the music images to the front of a plain paper cover. Add ric rac and ribbon trims then tie ribbon bows for a binding accent. Make a special opener by attaching a tiny box handle to the front.

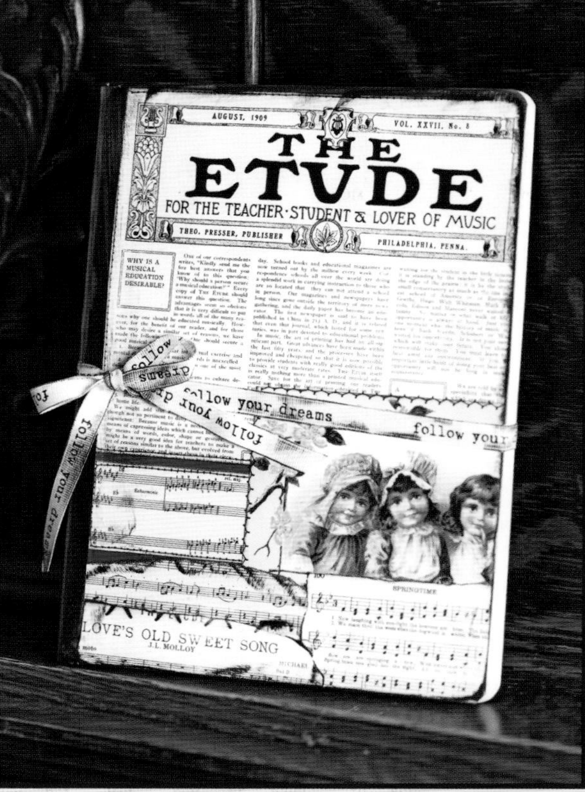

Idea 8

An Altered Art Composition Book is easy to make and a wonderful gift. Cut the desired image to fit the front cover of the book. Decoupage the image in place then tie a ribbon around the book as if it were a wrapped package.

Idea 9

A Baby Girl Altered Book is a wonderful gift for a new member of the family. Take an old baby book and decoupage the cover with selected images, game pieces, old buttons, and fabric cutouts. Pictures of the mother, the grandmother, and the great-grandmother can be added to the pages inside while plenty of room is still available for the new baby's pictures.

Idea 10

Create this Christmas card by folding a piece of card-stock in half. Using paper adhesive, adhere a Christmas music piece to the front of the card. Embellish with decorative ribbons, pieces of lace, and other memorabilia.

Idea 11

Old CDs should never be thrown away – use them as the base for Christmas ornaments. Print two images onto card-stock and cut to fit CD. Adhere using paper adhesive, smoothing carefully to eliminate any wrinkles. Punch a small hole in the top of the CD and tie a ribbon hanger.

SONG
LYRIC BY EDWIN STANLEY
MUSIC BY SOL. P LEVY
60
VAN DOORN MORGAN
FORSTER
MUSIC PUBLISHER INC.
736 SO. MICHIGAN AVE
CHICAGO
NEW YORK
N.Y.

MUS01-02

MUS01-03

MUS01-04

MUS01-05

MUS01-01

ff marcato
p elegante

THE ETUDE
FOR THE TEACHER STUDENT
AND LOVER OF MUSIC

MUS02-03

MUS02-02

MUS02-06

MUS02-04

MUS02-01

MUS02-05

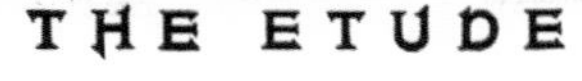

THE ETUDE

VIOLIN DEPARTMENT

CONDUCTED BY GEORGE LEHMANN.

Ignorance of the future makes life endurable. However great the pleasures or the honors which may be in store for us, if in knowing them we should be made aware of all the circumstances preceding, accompanying and following, we should experience a sense of disillusion. Hope would lose its charm, imagination its wings and the motives to noble effort their spring.
—*Bishop Spalding.*

BRATED
NCELLOS.

THE 'cello is such an important member of the violin family, that our readers cannot fail to be interested in the following of fine instruments (a number of them peared some time ago in our es- *The Strad.* rticle, T. A. W. Trowell, has

Wilhorsky, as a royal donation. Wilhorsky used this instrument nearly his whole life, but in his old age he abandoned music, and having no longer any need for the instrument, presented it to the solo violoncellist in the Czar's Court Orchestra, Franz Knecht, who made this entry into his diary (Oct. 30, 1850): "To-day Count Wilhorsky presented me with *the* Amati violoncello." Knecht used this instrument up till

felt he could not t
so after expressing
take it away at o
to him,
have

F. D. WRIGHT,
CLOTHING,
With
ARNOLD,
16 & 18 N. Salina Street,
SYRACUSE, N.Y.

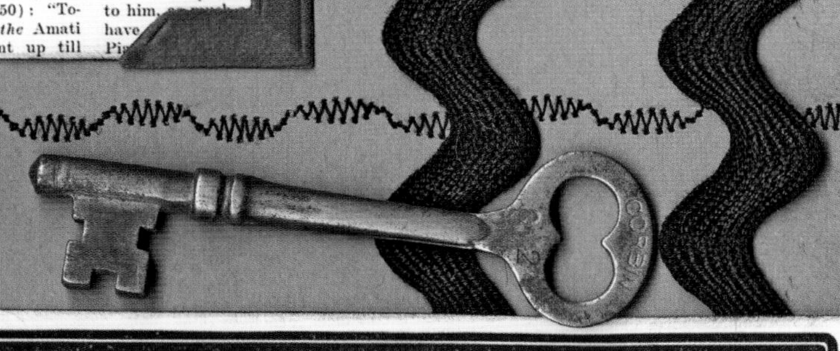

CALL AND SEE OUR
Three Large Stores,
Full of Choice Goods.
DAVIS BRO'S, Drugs and Fancy Goods,
LANSING.

THE ONLY NEW VIOLIN WITH THE TRUE OLD ITALIAN TONE

Lyon & Healy CREMONATONE Violins are made under the sunny skies of southern Europe by the foremost ng Italian and French Violin-makers, in shops under our exclusive control.

The CREMONATONE compares very favorably with the best of the old Italian instruments in tone quality. s result is obtained (1) *By using the best old Italian wood, garret-seasoned for more than a century; By reproducing the best examples of the work of Stradavari and Guarnerius;* (3) *By using a soft oil rnish from a recipe undoubtedly the same as that of the old masters;* (4) *By extending the varnishing d drying-out process over a period of from two to five years.*

We are thus able to offer a new Violin of smooth, even tone that becomes sweeter and more flexible with every nth of use. We have long been known as the world's leading dealers in high-grade Violins, our annual sales ng from 20,000 to 30,000 Violins. The CREMONATONE is the result of more than 40 years' experience and is ked by the reputation of this house.

No. G 1125. *A reproduction of the famous King Joseph Guarnerius, of the Hawley collection, ently sold by us for $12,000—broad, sweet tone. Sold on easy monthly payments,* **$100.00.**

NOTE.—Professionals who have spaired of ever obtaining a satisfacry Violin outside of the limited stock high-priced old ones, are cordially quested to order a CREMONATONE n seven days **free trial.**

84 Adams St., Chicago.

FREE Write today for a FREE copy of the new Lyon & Healy Musical Hand-book. Contains color-types of Lyon & Healy Cremonatone Violins. 300 pages, illustrations, prices and descriptions of over 25,000 Musical Instruments, all of good quality.

MUS03-03

MUS03-02

MUS03-04

MUS03-05

MUS03-07

MUS03-06

MUS03-01

Sweet Remembrance.
878
THE JOLLY COBBLER
Allegretto M.M. ♩= 104
FREDERICK A. WILLIAMS, Op. 70, No. 1
tap, tap, tap,
Here's the good cob - bler who works in his
Who could cut patch - es as neat - ly as
CODA
WEARING APPAREL
105
DOLGE SHOES
"VICTORIA"
BROWN
GREEN
RED
DRAB
BLACK
ALL SIZES
2.50 Delivered
A TREAT FOR YOUR FEET
"ON A FELT FOOTING"
DOLGE FELT
RICHLY FUR-BOUND
BEAUTIFULLY MADE
NOISELESS SOLES
& CO.
119 W.
NEW YORK
84
The Shoemaker
rap - a - tap, rap - a - tap, rap - a - tap - tap.
tic - a - tac, tic - a - tac, tic - a - tac - tac.

MUS04-03

MUS04-02

MUS04-04

MUS04-09

MUS04-08

MUS04-07

MUS04-05

MUS04-06

MUS04-01

p
rit.
mf

MUS05-03

MUS05-02

MUS05-04

MUS05-07

MUS05-06

MUS05-05

MUS05-01

rit.

MUS06-03

MUS06-02

MUS06-04

MUS06-010

MUS06-05

MUS06-09

MUS06-08

MUS06-06

MUS06-07

MUS06-01

Superior Ed.
(Schönen Blauen Donau)
Waltz
JOHANN STRAUSS, Op. 314
Tempo di Valse
THE ETUDE
Presser's Musical Magazine
OCTOBER 1921

MUS07-03

MUS07-02

MUS07-06

MUS07-04

MUS07-05

MUS07-01

The Improved Victor
the fifth
Loud enough for dancing
Victor Talking Machine Co. Philadelphia.
Sing with words.
1 2 3 3 4 3 2—2 3 4 4 5 4 3
Let us sing a lit - tle song, Time will quickly pass a - long,
4 3 2 3 4 5 6—5 4 3 4 3 2 1
Nev - er mind how long the day, Singing makes it fly a - way.
1 2 3 4 5 4 3—4 5 6 6 5 4 3
2 3 4 5 6 6 5—5 4 3 4 3 2 1
3 4 5 5 6 6 5—6 5 4 4 5 4 3
4 3 2 3 4 5 6—5 4 3 2 1 2 1
5 5 6 5 5 4 3—4 5 6 5 4 3 2
2 3 4 4 3 4 5—6 6 5 4 3 2 1

MUS08-02

MUS08-03

MUS08-04

MUS08-05

MUS08-01

Children's Page

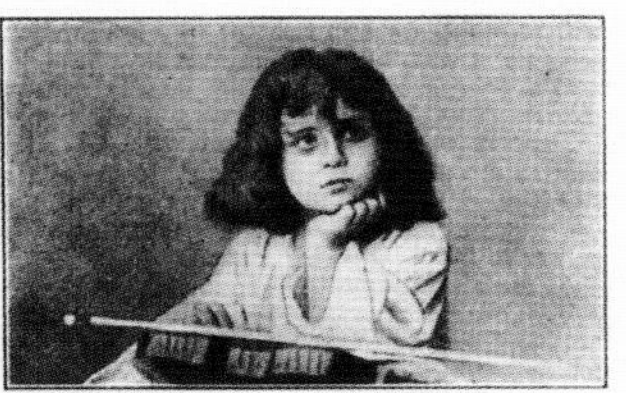

A Little Violinist.

LOVE FOR CHILDREN.

Whenever I see a bright-eyed boy or sweet-faced little girl I say to myself: "God bless you, dear child, and make your life one of use to your
fellows." All the duties and responsibilities of the
future rest on the dear children we see around us day
by day, at their little tasks, their innocent play, un-
conscious of the work that is preparing for them.
...eep in mind that life can have no more
...us than to prepare our little pupils
...e work of the world in the days to

music, drills, etc., are valuable in class work with children.

* * *

SCHUMANN'S DREAM BAIRNS.

The following is a very pretty weaving of the titles of some of Schumann's pieces into a connected form. Take the *Jugend Album* and *Kinderscenen* and see how many pieces you can find.

"From foreign parts" they come. There are some strong, and pink-cheeked, with puckered brows, and wide-open, smiling lips; listening, all ears and eyes, to a "funny story." Some tales are "frightening," and tiny hands search for big palms, and little fingers entwine with strong ones, while golden heads are pressed tight against the story-teller's knees. There are others, slight and fragile-looking, "almost too solemn" in appearance, with earnest, serious gaze, as if anticipating some wonderful, "important event." There is an "entreating child" with sweet, upturned, beseeching eyes; hoping, waiting, for its poor broken toy; the plaything, mended and whole again, is given him, and he seizes it, "quite happy" once more. Then there is a great game of blind man's buff, and "catch me if you can" is echoed from one to the other—all join in pursuit except one little man, who sits proudly like a "knight" astride his gaily painted "hobby horse." At last "by the fireside" the small crowd of

"Grease it," pron
"What do you do
"Oil the hinges."
"Our fingers run
voice sound hoarse
"I do not know."
"We have an oil for
must be used every day;
day and none the next, b
day. Do you think you
cry and sing if your finge
Herman went to the fair
terested in the horse-racing
next lesson, he enjoyed tell
had won the race. I deter
sity of practicing his exer
mind.
"And suppose that Bla
master: 'I know I am to e
going to practice running
want to win, quite as muc
learn, but I do not want
more than some children
music. I think it will be
me to run only once.' Do
won such honors? Now,
may call them ten little ho
as much as Black Harry t
After that, he tried to u
succeeded. His interest s
and as he slowly adva
rendering his little se
The last five min
in showing him pie
stories of their ch
the child's acquain
he can appreciate
before ...
Aud...

Answers to Violin Questions

I. R.—The subject of attuning
sonance boards of the violin is
ing world-wide attention just at
, and there is much discussion
any theories on the subject.
the top and back are removed
violin you can find their pitch
iking them with the knuckles.
piece of wood, as you know,
forth a definite musical note,
according to its size and den-

very difficult to secure data in
to the system of tuning the
of the violin as used by Stradi-
Herr Franz Niederheitmann, of
urg, Germany, a recognized
an authority, says: "With re-
o many Italian violins, it has
been ascertained that on their
aken apart, and the top as well
back hung suspended in the air
ck, the individual tones of both
by one-fifth exactly, the tone
e back sounding five tones higher
n that of the top. This is probably
nded on calculation and was the in-
tion of the old masters."
According to this authority if the
k was tuned to C the top would
tuned a fifth lower, that is to F
ural.

elbow is close to the side, it is gradua
raised in bowing on the A, D and
strings. While bowing on the G stri
the elbow is considerably raised, a
some eminent players raise their elb
nearly if not quite to the level of t
shoulder when playing a passage
the G string. An eminent authority
the German school, as taught
Joachim, says on this subject: "If
proper distance of the arm from
body is maintained, the elbow will
ways remain lower than the hand, a
the up-stroke has carried the hand
yond the point where it is in a l
with the forearm; this is an essen
thing, for to raise the elbow hig
than the hand disturbs the even pr
sure of the bow upon the strings, a
is a grievous fault. In bowing on
G string, the arm should be depres
about 20 degrees below a line dra
across and extending beyond
shoulders."
As you will see, this authority co
siders it a great error to allow the
bow to rise to the level of the should
It is an error which is frequently se
even in performers of considera
note. The tremolo should not be u
too much. Its effectiveness is grea
increased if it is only used where t
character of the music demands it.

Conducted by GEORGE LEHMANN

GRADING STUDENTS

In many schools and colleges it is the custom to give to the president, at the close of each term, the grades of pupils. These are sent to parents. As
a rule, I do not grade students high the first term,
even if they have studied with me before and are
perfectly familiar with my course of study. All pupils
...quested to practice at least one hour a day, and
...d pupils practice three or four hours daily.
...e in America are students under such dis-
...and system as in our best schools and colleges.
...college in which I teach is only one of many
...h this rigid system is maintained. At 9
...re to practice for the first hour
... rooms being already assigned.

Practice	Mon	Tues	Wed	Thrs	Fri	Sat
	hour	hour	hour	hour	hour	hour
Technical work	$\frac{1}{2}$	$\frac{1}{2}$	$\frac{1}{2}$	$\frac{1}{2}$	(Lesson)	1
Studies	$\frac{1}{2}$	$\frac{1}{2}$	$\frac{1}{4}$	1	$\frac{1}{2}$	$\frac{1}{2}$
Ensemble Duos	$\frac{1}{2}$			$\frac{1}{2}$	1	$\frac{1}{2}$
Pieces	$\frac{1}{2}$	$\frac{1}{2}$	$\frac{1}{2}$	$\frac{1}{2}$	$\frac{1}{2}$	$\frac{1}{2}$
Total	2	$1\frac{1}{2}$ (Lesson)	$1\frac{1}{4}$	$2\frac{1}{2}$	$1\frac{1}{2}$	$2\frac{1}{2}$

Edith L. Winn.

VIOLINS OLD AND NEW

Teachers are constantly called upon to give advice in regard to the purchase of violins. In most cases, and rightly, too, the advice is to buy an old one. At the present time, however,

parts than is t
struments. Th
perhaps not th
after thirty yea
condition and q
There are many
instruments exactly a
accept any wood th
to the same thickness
treatment. If the wo
able, an excellent re
just as probable that
writer knows one ma
above plan. After t
two hundred and firs
sold it for eighty
second was so poor
dollars for it.
Other makers will
ness, fineness of grai
istics of the wood,
ingly, working the w
or thinner, as judgu
There lies the true
In my opinion a b
buying a new violin
rest assured that, in
will in a few years
that it may be fully
old one.—*William E.*

A NEW VIOL... AND AN OL... THEORY

MUS09-03

MUS09-02

MUS09-04

MUS09-05

MUS09-01

SONGS
OF
HAPPINESS
CAROLYN S. BAILEY
Music by
MARY B. EHRMANN

MUS10-03

MUS10-02

MUS10-04

MUS10-05

MUS10-01

"GO DO LIKEWISE."

BY ANNA S. WEST.

Compliments of the
FISCHER PIANO.

the piano very well, and who, from the time s a little girl, had studied with a good teacher. our little maid was about seven years of age, she to hunger for the real knowledge of music, r a word of "can't *I* study?" did any one but she got to work, child though she was. told me of how she would sit at the piano for at a time studying the notes in an old in- book, marking the letters over the notes as zzled them out, fixing them "tightly" in her As a result, today she is a remarkably quick and ant sight-reader, and when questioned as to how oes it, modestly tells of her experience in herself to read music. had struggles with "time," but persevered until ... when she was twelve years old; but yet, word at home about a teacher. Fortunately

which would not be congenial, and yet I hardly felt enough faith in my own ability to teach music, and that was all I could do which I truly felt would bring success." But she went to the public library, where there were plenty of books upon the subject o her heart, subscribed to THE ETUDE, so full pful hints to teachers, and how she read, and d, *and* practiced! In a short time she felt tent enough to announce to her friends that ished pupil's, and without any dishonest as-

panied in work with other vocal pupils, in pense for her own tuition, and now, for three she has acceptably filled the position of alto t in one of the large churches in the town where sides. s she "buried her talent," do you think? With derate amount of strength you can do the same, *will*, and so enjoy yourself, and also *pass on* usic which you love. Get to work, girls! "Go and do likewise" with *your* musical ability.

PRACTICAL IDEAS APPLIED TO THE TEACHING OF CHILDREN.

BY KATHARINE BURROWES.

II.

THE teaching of a class would naturally be somewhat different from that of an individual pupil. The blackboard would form an important part of it, some ... joy ... and ear-training, muscle work, and rhythmic movements would also be possible.

has most marks gets a star. At the end of the term the pupil who has received the greatest number of stars is given a little prize of trifling value. This plan not only arouses but sustains enthusiasm, and I believe every teacher would find it helpful.

After this mental exercise has been worked on for a while, some muscular work would be in order, and for this purpose the following wrist exercise would be suitable: Hold the arms at full length, forming almost a level line from the shoulders to the hands. Throw one, then This may moments. is a good There are ... come into arned the n of one he teacher ich a staff clef, and e one line octave, using whole notes to indicate them and beginning with one line C.

Then give each pupil a blank book or pad or part of a sheet of music paper, and let these notes with their letter-names be copied over and over again. While they are doing this the teacher might take the pupils in turn to the piano, and teach them to play the one finger exercise given below.

RIGHT HAND.

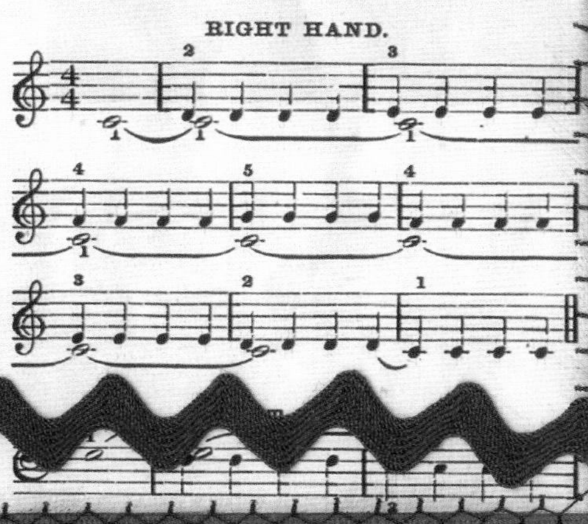

MUS11-02

MUS11-03

MUS11-04

MUS11-05

MUS11-01

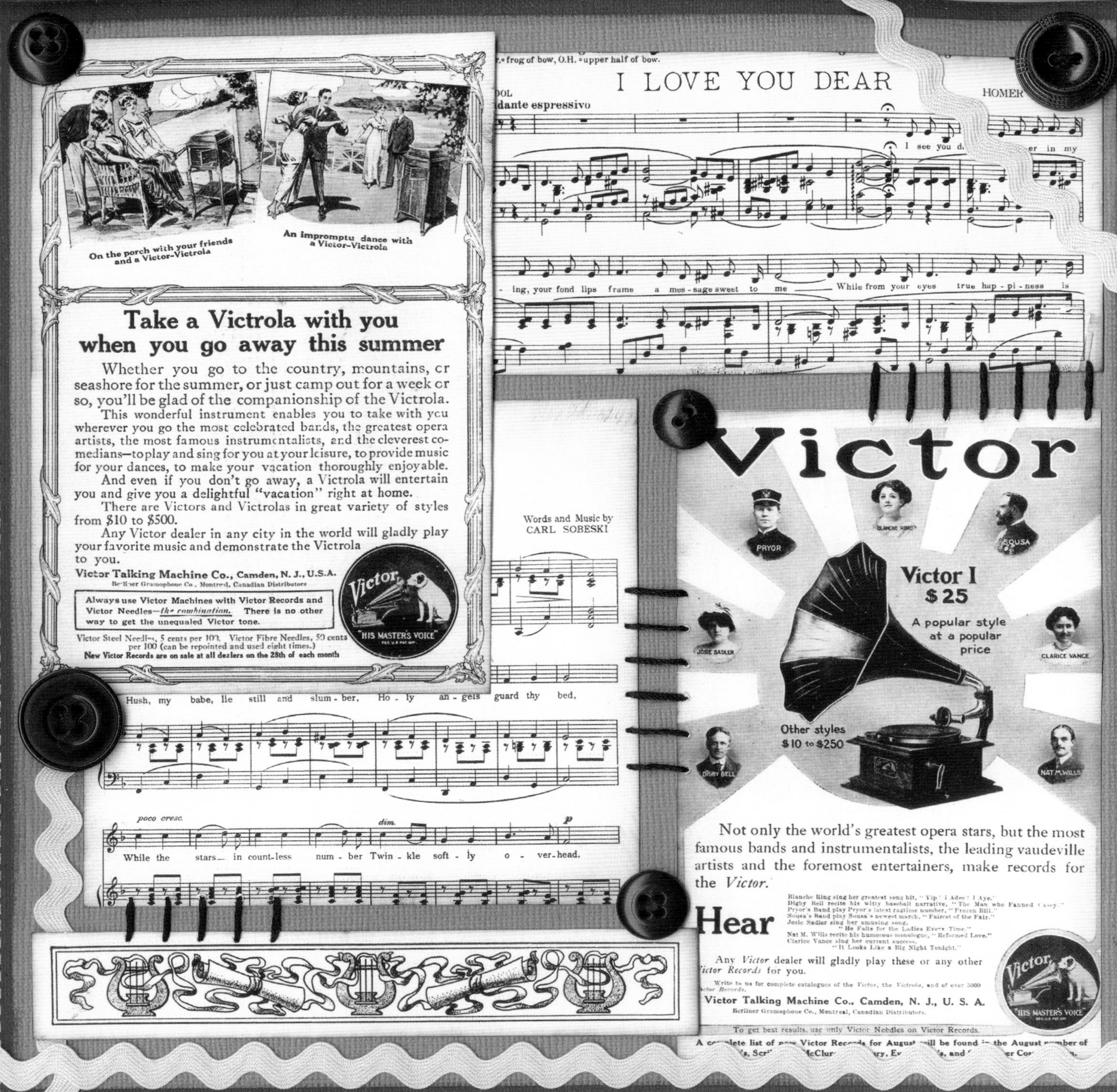
On the porch with your friends and a Victor-Victrola
An impromptu dance with a Victor-Victrola
Take a Victrola with you when you go away this summer
Whether you go to the country, mountains, or seashore for the summer, or just camp out for a week or so, you'll be glad of the companionship of the Victrola.
This wonderful instrument enables you to take with you wherever you go the most celebrated bands, the greatest opera artists, the most famous instrumentalists, and the cleverest comedians—to play and sing for you at your leisure, to provide music for your dances, to make your vacation thoroughly enjoyable.
And even if you don't go away, a Victrola will entertain you and give you a delightful "vacation" right at home.
There are Victors and Victrolas in great variety of styles from $10 to $500.
Any Victor dealer in any city in the world will gladly play your favorite music and demonstrate the Victrola to you.
Victor Talking Machine Co., Camden, N. J., U.S.A.
Berliner Gramophone Co., Montreal, Canadian Distributors
Always use Victor Machines with Victor Records and Victor Needles—the combination. There is no other way to get the unequaled Victor tone.
Victor Steel Needles, 5 cents per 100. Victor Fibre Needles, 50 cents per 100 (can be repointed and used eight times.)
New Victor Records are on sale at all dealers on the 28th of each month
Victor
"HIS MASTER'S VOICE"
frog of bow, O.H. = upper half of bow.
I LOVE YOU DEAR
HOMER
dante espressivo
I see you
ing, your fond lips frame a mes-sage sweet to me While from your eyes true hap-pi-ness is
Words and Music by
CARL SOBESKI
Hush, my babe, lie still and slum-ber, Ho-ly an-gels guard thy bed,
poco cresc.
dim.
While the stars in count-less num-ber Twin-kle soft-ly o-ver-head.
Victor
PRYOR
BLANCHE RING
SOUSA
Victor I
$25
A popular style at a popular price
JOSIE SADLER
CLARICE VANCE
Other styles
$10 to $250
DIGBY BELL
NAT M. WILLS
Not only the world's greatest opera stars, but the most famous bands and instrumentalists, the leading vaudeville artists and the foremost entertainers, make records for the Victor.
Hear
Blanche Ring sing her greatest song hit, "Yip! I Adee! I Aye."
Digby Bell recite his witty baseball narrative, "The Man who Fanned Casey."
Pryor's Band play Pryor's latest ragtime number, "Frozen Bill."
Sousa's Band play Sousa's newest march, "Fairest of the Fair."
Josie Sadler sing her amusing song, "He Falls for the Ladies Every Time."
Nat M. Wills recite his humorous monologue, "Reformed Love."
Clarice Vance sing her current success, "It Looks Like a Big Night Tonight."
Any Victor dealer will gladly play these or any other Victor Records for you.
Write to us for complete catalogues of the Victor, the Victrola, and of over 3000 Victor Records.
Victor Talking Machine Co., Camden, N. J., U. S. A.
Berliner Gramophone Co., Montreal, Canadian Distributors.
Victor
"HIS MASTER'S VOICE"
To get best results, use only Victor Needles on Victor Records.

MUS12-03

MUS12-02

MUS12-09

MUS12-04

MUS12-08

MUS12-07

MUS12-5

MUS12-06

MUS12-01

Snowflakes
See the lit-tle snow-flakes fall-ing White they lie up-on the ground Now the mer-ry
breez-es play-ing Scat-ter snow-flakes all a-round. Snow-flakes on the trees and bush-es
Deep in drifts they snug-ly lie Warm they keep the seeds and root-lets For the Spring-time bye and bye.
48
Ex. 58.
Win-ter's glittr'ing cloak of snow, Hides the seeds of life be-low.
II.
III.
Ex. 59.
Dark De-cem-ber's dreary night, Needs the grate-fire's blazing light.
II.
III.
LITTLE FLAKES OF SNOW.
1. We are lit-tle flakes of snow, In your windows glanc-ing,
2. Lit-tle flakes of fall-ing snow, Flit-ting hith-er, thith-er,
3. Oh we love the win-ter time, When to earth we're whirl-ing,
Here and there so light we go, Through the air a-danc-ing.
Flutt'ring, flutt'ring, down we go, No one knoweth whith-er.
Love the i-cy snow and rime, Banners white un-furl-ing.
THE SNOWFLAKES.
1. Down, down, down, down, Fall the pretty snow-flakes fall the pret-ty snow-flakes,
2. White, white, white, white, Cov-er they the meadows, cov-er they the meadows,
Down, down, down, down, Fall the pret-ty snowflakes on the frost-y ground.
White, white, white, white, Cover they the meadows and the leaf-less trees.

MUS13-03

MUS13-02

MUS13-07

MUS13-04

MUS13-06

MUS13-05

MUS13-01

THE New York State Music Teachers' Association met in Rochester, June 27th-29th, under the presidency of Mr. Jaroslaw de Zielinski, of Buffalo. The session opened on Tuesday morning with the reports of officers and other business matters, followed by a vocal recital. The afternoon was given up to organ recitals by Wilhelm Middelschulte, of Chicago, and Mary Chappel Fisher, of Rochester. In the evening, Rudolph Ganz, of Chicago, gave a piano recital. The morning session on Wednesday was given up to addresses and discussions on subjects connected with work in music in the public schools. In the afternoon, Mr. Edwin Lockhart, of New York City, gave a song recital and lecture, followed by a piano recital by Mme. Birdice Blye. The evening concert was given by Julian Walker, basso, Mrs. Eva Gardner Coleman, soprano, and Mr. Neidliska, violinist. On Thursday morning, business was again taken up and Geneva was selected as the place for holding the next meeting. Papers were read on vocal subjects by Miss A. J. Latham and Mr. J. D. Mehan, of New York City. The afternoon was given to social recreation; in the evening a lecture recital on the work of women composers, by Miss Mary Howard, of Buffalo, and the Harmonie Quartet, and a miscellaneous concert by Reed Miller, tenor, and Milada Czerny, pianist. The president for 1905-1906 is Mr. Carl G. Schmidt, of New York; Chairman of the Program Committee, Mr. Charles H. Farnsworth, of the Teachers' College, New York City.

THE house in which J. S. Bach was born at Eisenach has been purchased by the Bach Society and will be used as a Bach Museum.

JOACHIM, the violinist, recently celebrated his seventy-fourth birthday.

25 Glee or Chorus Books

At Introductory Rates (ONE Copy ONLY of each Book at this Sample Price)

	No.		Retail Price (1st Col.)	Special Price (2d Col.)
Quartets and Choruses for Male Voices	674	Decker's Collection of Part Songs for Male Voices (Partly Humorous)	$0.35	$0.15
	616	Glee Club Vol. 1 contains 22 Part Songs within the range of ordinary voices	.35	.15
	756	Glee Club Vol. 2 contains 21 Part Songs " " " " " "	.25	.15
	1048	Glee Club Vol. 3 contains 13 Part Songs. Highest note F sharp (Partly Humorous)	.25	.15
	659	Popular Songs Vol. 1 arranged for Male Voices by C. F. SHATTUCK	.35	.15
	857	Popular Songs Vol. 2 " " " " " C. F. SHATTUCK	.35	.15
	1580	Popular Songs Vol. 3 " " " " " C. F. SHATTUCK	.35	.15
	911	Popular Songs Vol. 2 " " " Quartet " WM. H. RIEGER	.35	.20
	497	Molineux' Collection of Sacred Music for Male Voices, not difficult, Vol. 1	.50	.20
	1293	Molineux' Collection of Sacred Music for Male Voices, not difficult, Vol. 2	.50	.20
	1294	Barrett's Collection of Sacred Music for Men's Voices, for Masonic and Church use	.60	.30
	714	Steele's Vocal Class Instruction Book for Men's Voices, including Easy Part Songs	.60	.30
	1292	Molineux' Humorous Selections for Male Voices, Vol. 1	.35	.15
	1602	Old Songs arranged for Male Quartet and Choruses, Vol. 1	.35	.15
	1603	Old Songs " " " " " " Vol. 2	.35	.15
Part Songs and Choruses for Mixed Voices	678	Molineux' Repertoire, Vol. 1, 13 Simple Part Songs for Mixed Voices	.25	.15
	725	Molineux' Repertoire, Vol. 2, 11 " " " " " "	.25	.15
	781	The Unique, Vol. 1, 13 Part Songs for Mixed Voices (48 pages)	.35	.15
	1291	The Unique, Vol. 2, 14 " " " " " (48 pages)	.35	.15
Sacred—Anthems, Etc.	361	Molineux' Sacred Gems, Vol. 1. Anthems of Good Grade (77 pages)	.50	.20
	728	Molineux' Collection of Glorias (13 settings)	.25	.15
	732	Trinity Collection of Anthems. By H. P. DANKS (85 pages)	.50	.25
School Songs	1581	Molineux' Songs for Schools and Seminaries	.25	.10
	....	Steele's Rote Songs for Primary Grade	.15	.10
Quartets for Female Voices	1582	Molineux' Collection of Quartets for Female Voices	.35	.15
		Total	$9.15	$4.25

WE OFFER THESE BOOKS at the special **low price** in the special offer column to induce you to **examine them.** You may select one Book or **one each** of any of these Books at the prices marked, and they will be sent, postage or express prepaid, upon receipt of the price in **right hand column.** Special price for one copy each of all the above 25 Books sent upon application.

Future Discount: Twenty per cent. or one-fifth from prices in first column. To which add postage.

With the exception of the **ROTE SONGS** and **No. 714,** all the music in these Books is also published separately in **Octavo Sheet** form. Prices in most cases will be found upon the covers. These prices in sheet form are subject to discount of 25 per cent.

MUS14-03

MUS14-02

MUS14-04

MUS14-05

MUS14-01

…y, if he will only give himself … …etely to art and to work."

TO THE CHILD WHO ONLY WANTS TO PLAY "DANCE MUSIC."

BY LEONORA SILL ASHTON.

THE one ambition of many children taking piano lessons is to learn two-steps, waltzes and marches. The reason for this is easy to see. The ear loves rhythm, and it is the clearly defined "catchy" movement of these pieces that makes them attractive to children.

If you love this kind of music, and it is easy for you to learn to play it, that is one of the surest proofs that you have a quick musical ear and a natural talent, but remember there are many different ways of writing music besides the dance forms. Let us see if we cannot find something in thes… as interesting and enjoyable as in th… two-steps and waltzes.

Marches and dances are created for the distinct purpose of exciting

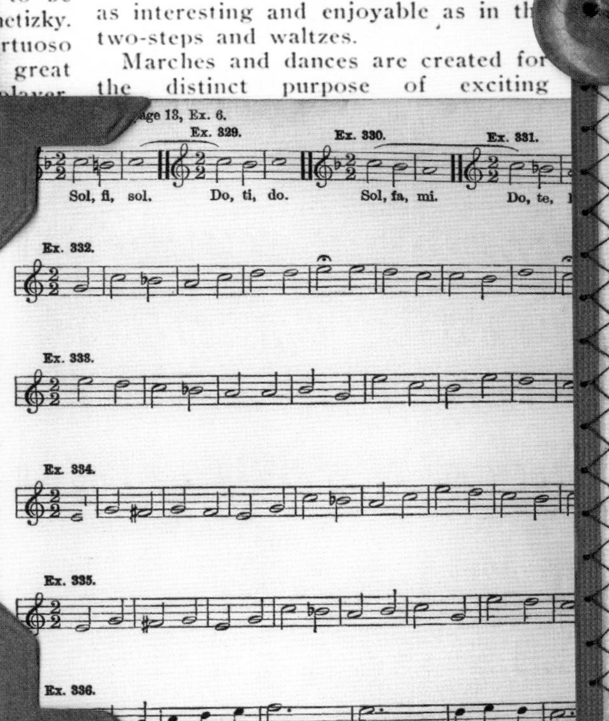

MUS15-03

MUS15-02

MUS15-06

MUS15-04

MUS15-05

MUS15-01

Five-finger
fingers to lateral security.
thumb exercise.
For sliding fingers.
For speed.
ng the tonograph, carry them into other keys.
n all keys.
s are scale numbers.
The position o
WEBER
PIANO
The distinguishing characte
istic of the Weber Piano is its
Sympathetic Tone;
that is because it is constructed
from the Musician's Standpoint.
WAREROOMS:
Fifth Ave., cor. 16th Street, New-York.
258-260 Wabash Ave., Chicago.
511 Wood St., Pittsburg.
Masonic Temple, Denver.
Con moto
A frog he
Wheth-er his moth-er would let him or
Gam-mon and
FROM OLDEN DAYS
Transcriptions
for
Violin and Pianoforte
by
ALFRED MOFFAT
F. Ainé _ Promenade .50.
Joseph Agus _ Larghetto espressivo .40.
Fernando d'Almeyda _ Menuett in G .50.
Giuseppe Tartini _ Adagio sostenuto .40.
M. de Guillon _ Romanza in D .50.
BOSTON, 120, Boylston Street
ARTHUR P. SCHMIDT.
LEIPZIG, Lindenstrasse 16
NEW YORK, 11 West 36th Street
Copyright 1913 by Arthur P. Schmidt
International Copyright Secured
THE ETUDE
THE NILES BRYANT
hool of Piano Tuning
MUSIC HALL
PIANO TUNING PAYS.
The Tune-a-Phone in Use.
a gras
in which
the one I wish
being, the "musica
estatic and soul-thrilling i
and even those whose souls are thri
watha" are barred.
What is it to be musical? In the
this is meant a state of mind, of devel
tain mental possibilities or capabilities
go as far as the Blavatskyites and say
self is merely a state of mind; di
should have to continue along this
the instruments that make music are
that they have no material existence
A primary condition of being mu
having a strong feeling for rhythm
innate or it may be cultivated from
the necessary strength. The mather
tion of rhythm may be accurate; a person
curately explain all subdivisions of a measu
yet not be able to play that measure "in time."
clock-work of the brain does not act wi
dulum. But this may be ove
I have seen it
Piano News
We are ready to send
copy of our beautiful
Piano Book
free of charge to your
address. This book con-
tains illustrations in colors
of the leading makes of
pianos of the present time,
and should be in the hands
of everyone contemplating
the purchase of an instrument. We quote lowest
Chicago prices, and can
save you $50 or more.
Besides you have the advan-
tage of a selection from the
World's Largest
and most
Varied Stock
24 Leading
We also include a copy of our 12-page Bargain List
New Upright Pianos, $125 to 300 and upwards. Good Used Pianos
of several hundred, Squares $50; Uprights $100 and upward.
ranged. We ship Pianos everywhere. Schedule of Freigh
LYON
HEALY,

MUS16-04

MUS16-03

MUS16-02

MUS16-07

MUS16-05

MUS16-06

MUS16-01

MUS16-05

SAYING MY A B C

"A, b, c, d, e, f, g;
H, i, j, k, l, m, n, o, p;
Q, r, s and t, u, v;
W, x and y and z.
Now I've said my A B C,
Tell me what you think of me."

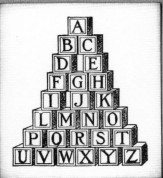

TWINKLE, TWINKLE, LITTLE STAR.
SECOND AND THIRD VERSES.
When the blaz - ing sun is gone, When he no - thing shines up
Then the traveller in the dark Thanks you for your ti - ny
on, Then you show your lit - tle light, Twin-kle, twin-kle, all the night.
spark: How could he see where to go, If you did not twin-kle so?
poco rit.

Great A, little a,
Bouncing B.
The cat's in the cupboard
And she can't see.

MUS17-03

MUS17-02

MUS17-08

MUS17-07

MUS17-04

MUS17-05

MUS17-06

MUS17-01

CHAPTER IV.
LESSON 13.
89. When the tone B♭ is taken as key tone (1 or do), the KEY SIGNATURE will be TWO FLATS, one on the third line, and one in the fourth space, thus:
8 or 1.
1 or 8.
Ex. 55. Scale of B♭.
Ex. 56.
Upper Scale.
Ex. 57.
No-bly think, no-bly act in life's en-deav-or,
Show a will to dare and do, Be a cow-ard nev-er.
II.
III.
IV.
Girl: Who sings happy songs?
Boy: I sing happy songs.
45

MUS18-03

MUS18-02

MUS18-04

MUS18-05

MUS18-01

11. The *sign* for a tone lasting through one part of a measure or one beat is this: ♩, called a QUARTER NOTE.

12. If one part of a measure is to be silent it is shown by a *sign* like this: 𝄽 called a QUARTER REST.

Ex. 6.

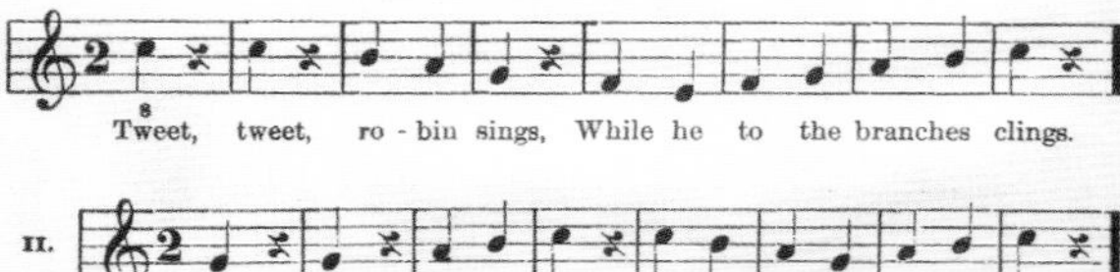

Tweet, tweet, ro - bin sings, While he to the branches clings.
II.

Sing again, happy girls.
Sing again, happy boys.
Sing, happy children.
Happy children, sing today.

Come, sing with me.
Sing with me, happy children.
Sing with me today.
Sing, happy children, sing.

33

Little bluebird in the tree,
Sing a song to me.

MUS19-02

MUS19-03

MUS19-04

MUS19-05

MUS19-01

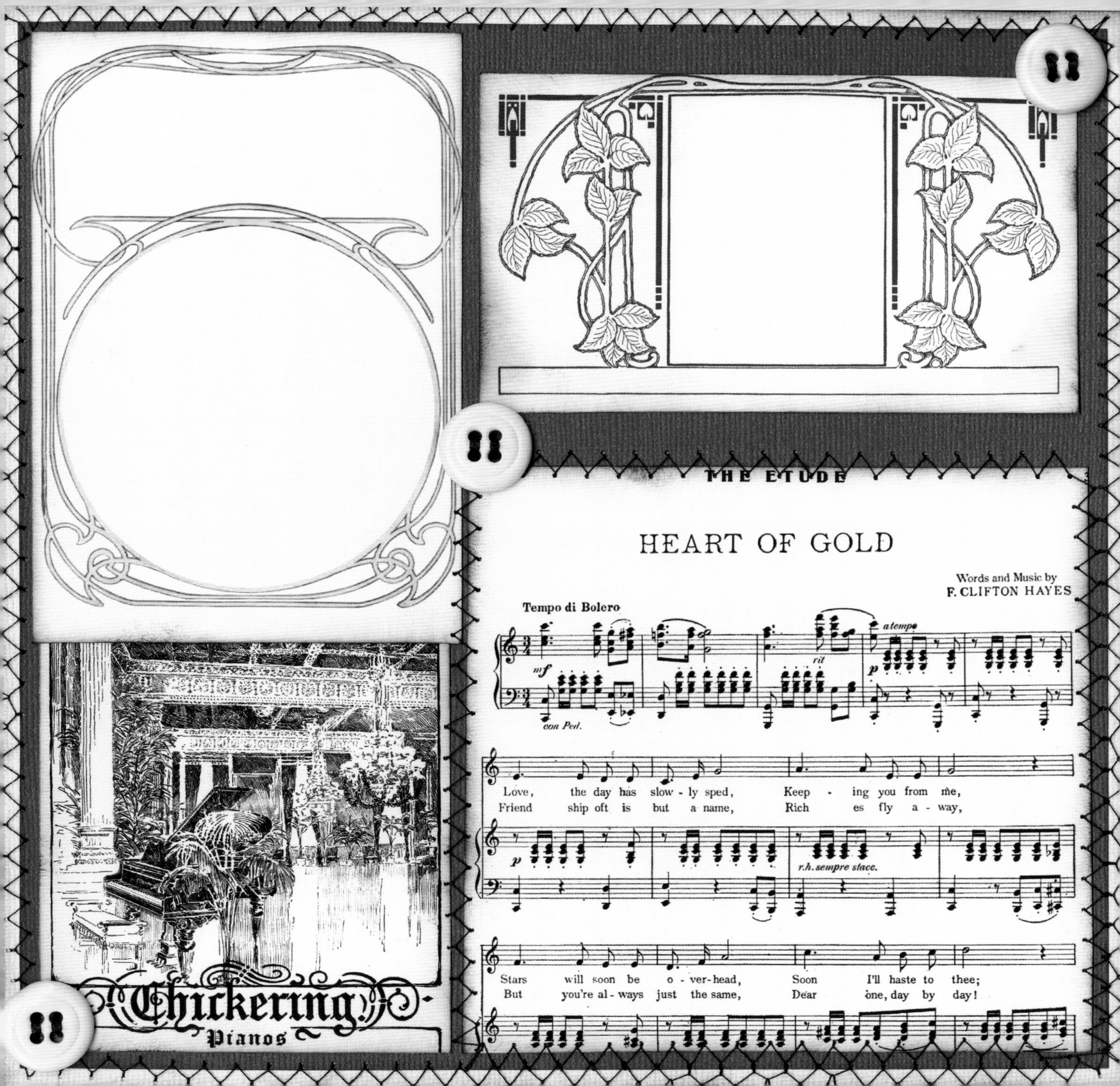

THE ETUDE
HEART OF GOLD
Words and Music by
F. CLIFTON HAYES
Tempo di Bolero
Love, the day has slow-ly sped, Keep - ing you from me,
Friend ship oft is but a name, Rich es fly a-way,
r.h. sempre stacc.
Stars will soon be o-ver-head, Soon I'll haste to thee;
But you're al-ways just the same, Dear one, day by day!
Chickering
Pianos

MUS20-03

MUS20-02

MUS20-06

MUS20-04

MUS20-05

MUS20-01

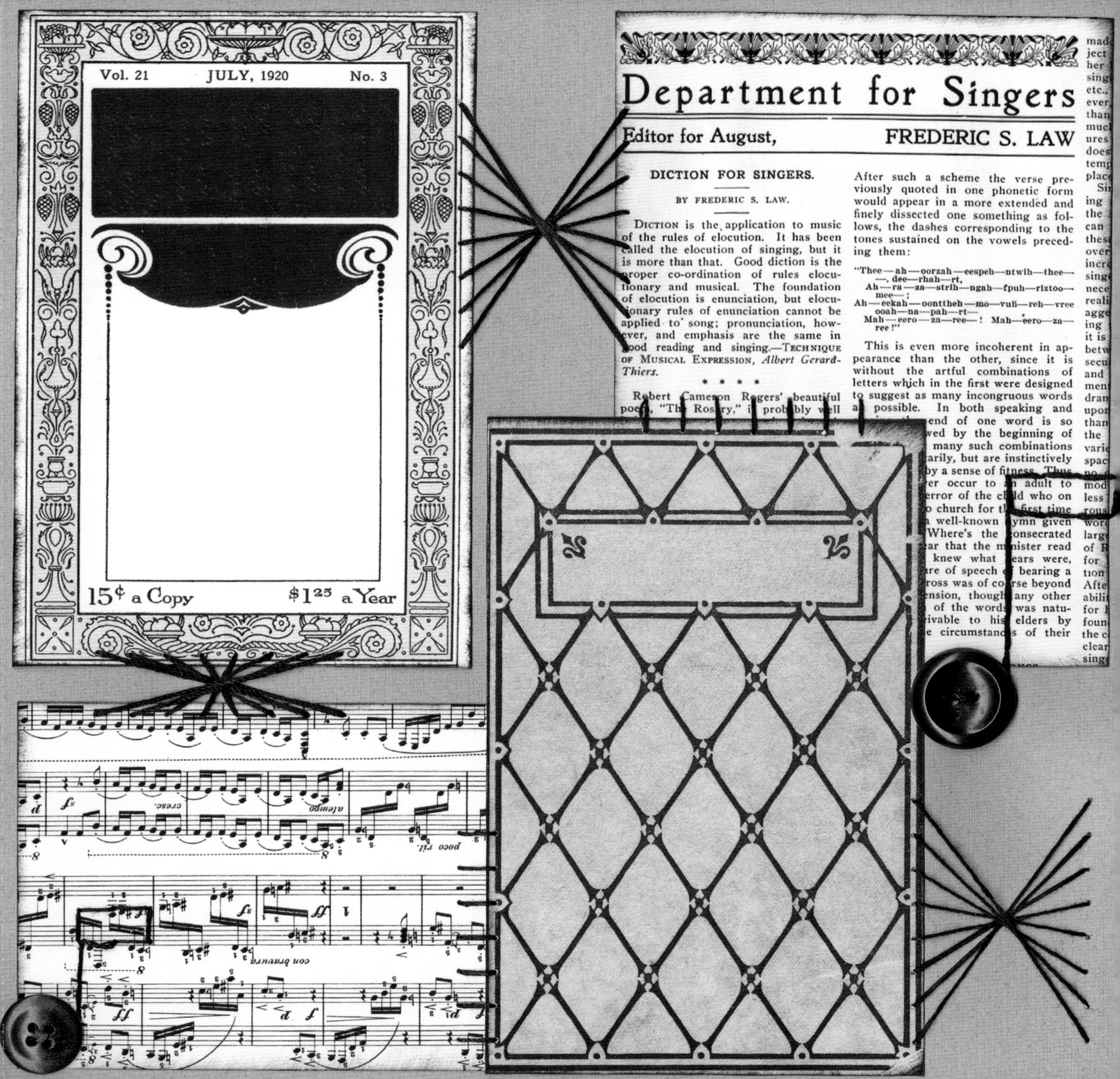

Vol. 21
JULY, 1920
No. 3
15¢ a Copy
$1.25 a Year
Department for Singers
Editor for August,
FREDERIC S. LAW
DICTION FOR SINGERS.
BY FREDERIC S. LAW.
DICTION is the application to music of the rules of elocution. It has been called the elocution of singing, but it is more than that. Good diction is the proper co-ordination of rules elocutionary and musical. The foundation of elocution is enunciation, but elocutionary rules of enunciation cannot be applied to song; pronunciation, however, and emphasis are the same in good reading and singing.—TECHNIQUE OF MUSICAL EXPRESSION, Albert Gerard-Thiers.
* * * *
After such a scheme the verse previously quoted in one phonetic form would appear in a more extended and finely dissected one something as follows, the dashes corresponding to the tones sustained on the vowels preceding them:
"Thee—ah—oorzah—eespeh—ntwih—thee——, dee—rhah—rt,
Ah—ra—za—strih—ngah—fpuh—rlztoo—mee—;
Ah—eekah—oonttheh—mo—vuli—reh—vree ooah—na—pah—rt—
Mah—eero—za—ree—! Mah—eero—za—ree!"
This is even more incoherent in appearance than the other, since it is without the artful combinations of letters which in the first were designed to suggest as many incongruous words as possible. In both speaking and
end of one word is so
wed by the beginning of
many such combinations
arily, but are instinctively
by a sense of fitness. Thus
er occur to an adult to
error of the child who on
church for the first time
a well-known hymn given
Where's the consecrated
ar that the minister read
knew what tears were,
re of speech of bearing a
ross was of course beyond
ension, though any other
of the words was natu-
eivable to his elders by
e circumstances of their
cresc.
a tempo
poco rit.
con bravura

MUS21-03

MUS21-02

MUS21-06

MUS21-04

MUS21-05

MUS21-01

Fifth.
Fifth.
Ex. 79.
See saw, see saw, up in the air we go;
High up, high up and down, down low.
Key of F.
II.
Key of G.
III.
Key of A.
IV.
Sing with scale names, singing names, la and koo.
Ex. 7.
I. 1 2 3 4 5 6 5—6 5 4 3 2 2 1—
II. 1 2 3 3 4 5 6—5 6 5 4 3 2 1—
III. 1 2 3 4 3 4 5—6 6 5 4 3 2 1—
IV. 1 2 1 2 3 3 4—5 6 5 4 3 2 1—
V. 1 2 3 2 3 4 5—6 5 5 4 3 2 1—
VI. 3 3 4 3 2 3 4—5 6 5 4 3 2 1—
VII. 3 4 5 5 6 6 5—4 4 3 3 2 2 1--
VIII. 3 2 3 4 5 6 5—6 5 5 4 3 2 1—
IX. 5 5 6 6 5 4 3—4 5 4 3 2 2
X. 5 6 5 4 3 4 5—6 5 4 3 2 2

MUS22-03

MUS22-02

MUS22-04

MUS22-07

MUS22-05

MUS22-06

MUS22-01

51
meno mosso
Vivo
HEARTY
GREETING
With
affectionate wishes
for your happiness
in the
NEW YEAR

MUS23-04

MUS23-03

MUS23-02

MUS23-05

MUS23-06

MUS23-01

To Mr. & Mrs. Wm. J. MacFarland, Philada., Pa.
2
LOVE AND DEVOTION.
(MEDITATION)
LOUIS A. DRUMHELLER, Op
Ped.
p
No 5031
LOVE DREAMS
REVERIE.
Very slow.
A. L. BROWN.
espressivo
legato
pp
R. H.
L. H.

MUS24-03

MUS24-02

MUS24-04

MUS24-05

MUS24-07

MUS24-01

MUS24-06

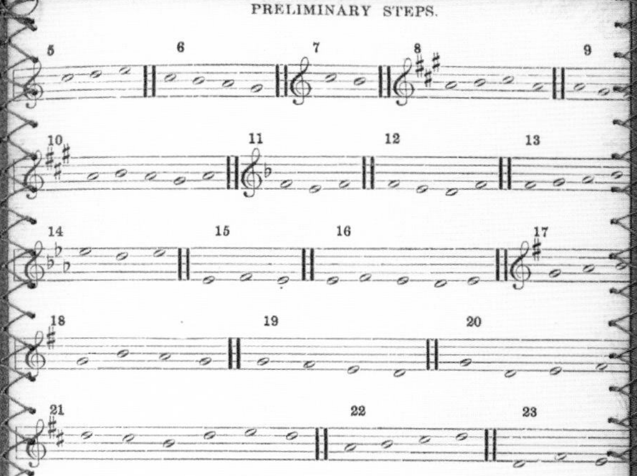

PRELIMINARY STEPS.

The teacher will readily perceive how the exercises may be inf
varied, but she must have some definite point to establish with
lesson. This will be suggested to her by the chart exercise. For in
if the chart exercise is a study of *Sol*, Sol may become the c
interest in the dictation exercise, and by following in a general w
exercise on the chart she will establish the point. She should, ho
not be guided by the position given to Sol in the chart exercise, but s
vary the position constantly.

In a single lesson three or four examples are sufficient. Th

Sing, happy children.
It is spring.
Sing, happy bluebird,
Bring glad news.

55

WHAT IT MEANS TO BE MUSICAL.

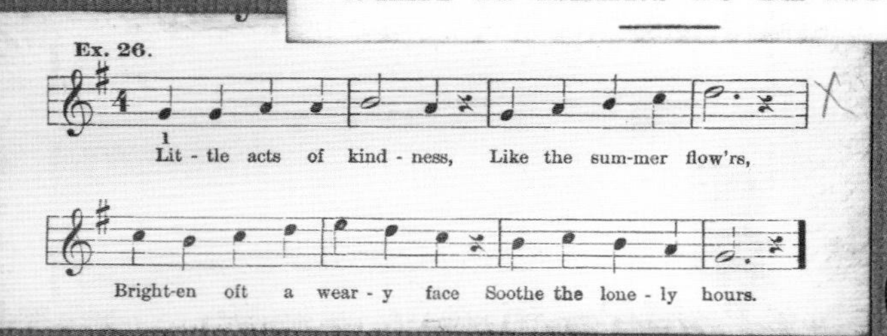

Ex. 26.
Lit - tle acts of kind - ness, Like the sum-mer flow'rs,
Bright-en oft a wear - y face Soothe the lone - ly hours.

MUS25-03

MUS25-02

MUS25-04

MUS25-08

MUS25-07

MUS25-05

MUS25-06

MUS25-01

FREDERIC LILLEBRIDGE, Executive Editor
DR. W. S. B. MATHEWS, Editor
EMIL SAUER, Co-
FLAT SCALES, FOR BOTH HANDS.
from C.
D flat.
A flat
THE EVERETT PIANO
¶ Every appeal we make for consideration of this piano is caused by its compelling attributes—principally its superior tone distinction—its tone carrying capacity or vibration—its power, and its singing quality.
¶ Constant striving for the best in tone is the secret of our success therein.
¶ Everett Tone is tone that Compels.
¶ This definite attribute upholds Everett sovereignty among pianos.
THE JOHN CHURCH COMPANY
CINCINNATI NEW YORK CHICAGO
Owners of the Everett Piano Co., Boston
8. Each measure is made out of one strong tone or part
more weak tones, or parts.
9. The number of parts in a measure is shown by the
the beginning; the number 2 meaning two parts in a me
Ex. 4.
10. The number of parts in a measure may also be sh
called BEATING TIME. The motions for two parts in a
strong part, up for the weak part.
Ex. 5.
D U D U D U D U D U D
IVERS & POND
PIANOS
The beautiful new model here illustrated has been called the daintiest and most charming upright we have ever made. Designed on Louis XV lines by an artist of national repute, it offers a graceful medium between the severe and the over ornate. Musically and structurally nothing finer can be had. Ivers & Pond
experience of half a century of fine piano-
New Model. Style 605.
Embodying the latest improvements and the last word in case-designing.
"For Thirty-five Years a Standard Piano"
THE WING PIANO
From the Factory at Wholesale Price
We make the Wing Piano and sell it ourselves. It goes direct from our factory to your home. We do not employ any agents or salesmen, and do not sell through dealers or retail stores. When you buy the Wing Piano you pay the actual cost of making it and our one small wholesale profit. This profit is small because we sell thousands of pianos yearly. Most retail stores sell no more than twelve to twenty pianos yearly and must charge from $100 to $200 profit on each. Think for yourself; they cannot help it.
Save from $100 to $200
SENT ON TRIAL
WE PAY FREIGHT
NO MONEY IN ADVANCE
We will send any Wing Piano to any part of the United States on trial. We pay freight in advance and do not ask for any advance payment or deposit. If the piano is not satisfactory after twenty days' trial in your home, we take it back entirely at our expense.
Old instruments taken in exchange.
EASY MONTHLY PAYMENTS
45 Styles to select from
Wing Pianos are guaranteed for twelve years against any defect in tone, action, workmanship or material.
Other Piano
Prominent Purchasers
You Need This Book
umental Attachment
Wing Organs
Years Over 36,000 Pianos
ING & SON
518–520 West 13th Street, New York City
For Piano Students
Kursheedt's HAND EXPANDER
A Necessity for all Musicians.
Price $3.50
By Express 25 cents Extra.
E. B. KURSHEEDT,
10 Bleecker Street, New York City, N. Y.
HOME, SWEET HOME.
VAR.

MUS26-04 MUS26-03 MUS26-02

MUS26-05 MUS26-08

MUS26-06 MUS26-07

MUS26-01

Try the Cornish Plan.

If you don't know what it is write us about it to-day. We will send it free, together with our most beautiful Souvenir Album, our elegant colored and embossed miniature pianos and organs and full particulars of the free musical education we give to every purchaser of either a piano or organ.

THE CORNISH PLAN is the easiest, simplest on earth. It tells how we sell pianos and organs direct from the factory to the customer at wholesale, factory-cost price. Easy payments, too, if you say so.

THE EMBOSSED MINIATURES are exact reproductions in color and style of some of our leading styles of pianos and organs. They show just how our instruments will look in your own home and will greatly aid you in making a desirable selection.

THE ELEGANT SOUVENIR ALBUM is the finest example of the printer's art ever sent out by any piano or organ manufacturers in the world. It shows 50 different styles of pianos and organs and is our only solicitor; no agent or dealer will worry you; you can see exactly what we have for sale, and every instrument is marked in plain figures at lowest factory cost. You know just what a Cornish piano or organ will cost you Cash or Credit, and we have a scale to suit all pockets and any circumstances.

CORNISH

PIANOS and ORGANS

Factory to Home

Most Liberal Offer Ever Made.

To every purchaser of one of our instruments we give absolutely free a certificate entitling the holder to a **two years' scholarship** in the United States School of music. This is the most satisfactory plan of home education ever devised. Success is certain. You cannot fail with it. Full particulars with Album.

Try one of our pianos for one year. We send them anywhere. No money required in advance. If you find it not as represented send it back at our expense. We will pay the freight both ways and 6 per cent interest on your money. No better offer was ever made. Cornish pianos can't be excelled in touch, tone, style or finish. Been selling pianos and organs this way for 50 years, and not one has ever come back as unsatisfactory. We sell high-grade organs on the same plan. We make all our instruments and sell them direct to users. We guarantee to save you half the price and give a free musical education.

YOUR CREDIT IS GOOD UNDER THE CORNISH PLAN.

Over quarter of a million of Cornish pianos and organs are in use. Every one of them is noted for its style, tone, touch, quality and finish. We can show you one or more in your own town in use from 1 to 25 years in most cases. Don't take our word for it. We are willing to trust you. Try either a piano or organ at our expense. You don't pay for anything unless you keep it. If you want it, any reasonable easy payment plan will meet our approval. Send for one now.

How Some People Buy: Some people buy a piano or organ for the case—they want fine furniture; some buy for the name of the maker—they want to gratify vanity; some buy for the fineness of tone—they want good music. You are sure of all these and more in buying a Cornish. You simply cannot make a mistake. They are the highest possible grade and built to last a lifetime, and the prices will surprise you.

Don't buy a piano or organ of any kind until you receive our new special Souvenir Album and Embossed Miniatures. The Album contains the most astonishing price offerings ever heard of and the most liberal offers ever made. Write for them to-day and you will receive descriptions of 50 different styles to select from, all at wonderful prices. Lay this McCall down and write now. If you neglect it you are likely to forget about it. Address

CORNISH CO. Washington, New Jersey.

172 ADVERTISEMENTS.

TEN SETS REEDS.

Fine Walnut Case.
Height, 75 ins.
Depth, 46 ins.
Width, 24 ins.

BEATTY'S {27 Stops} ORGANS

If you are about to buy a PARLOR ORGAN, purchase the latest resonant walnut Case, Beatty's BEETHOVEN Cabinet Organ, Now Ready, by far the best for the least money. Proof, shipping one every ten minutes. TEN Sets Reeds, viz:—
1 Charming Saxaphone,
2 Famous French Horn,
3 Beautiful Piccolo Reeds
4 Jubilante-Violina,
5 Powerful Sub-Bass,
6 Sweet Voix Celeste,
7 Soft Cello Reeds,
8 Dulcinna Reeds,
9 Diapason Reeds,
10 Clarionet Reeds.

27 Useful Stops,

including Sub-Bass, Octave Coupler, Voix Celeste, etc. Producing 14 Combinations equal to 14 ordinary organs combined also, Compass Regulator, a new invention just added. Price, $125.00, offered now as a MIDSUMMER HOLIDAY OFFER with Bench, Book and Music, for

ONLY $65.00

so as to introduce quickly. I am very busy; no time to write more about this beautiful parlor organ in this advertisement. What I want is for you to send me $65.00, thus ordering the best Cabinet Organ. Its introduction is far better than anything that can be written, the instrument speaks for itself, it sings its own praises. Money refunded, with interest, if not as represented after one year's use. Nothing saved by correspondence.

VISITORS WELCOME

Any person who will call and select organ in person, $5.00 will be deducted for traveling expenses.

ADVERTISEMENTS. 485

BEATTY ORGANS AND PIANOS.

ORDER NOW for CHRISTMAS PRESENTS.

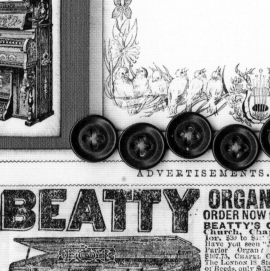

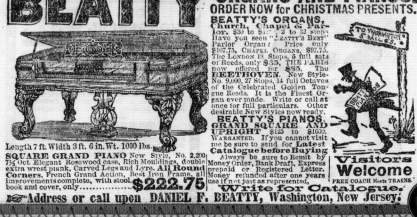

BEATTY'S ORGANS, Church, Chapel & Parlor, $30 to $1000. 2 to 32 stops Have you seen "BEATTY'S BEST" Parlor Organ? Price only $107.75, CHAPEL ORGANS, $97.75. The LONDON 18 Stops, 5 full sets of Reeds, only $65, THE PARIS now offered for $85. The **BEETHOVEN.** New Style No. 9,000, 27 Stops, 14 full Octaves of the Celebrated Golden Tongue Reeds. It is the Finest Organ ever made. Write or call at once for full particulars. Other desirable New Styles now ready.

BEATTY'S PIANOS. GRAND SQUARE AND UPRIGHT $125 to $1600. WARRANTED. If you cannot visit me be sure to send for **Latest Catalogue before Buying**

Always be sure to Remit by Money Order, Bank Draft, Express prepaid or Registered Letter. Money refunded after one years use if not just as represented,

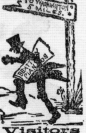

TO WASHINGTON 5 MILES.

Visitors Welcome

FREE COACH Meets TRAINS.

Length 7 ft. Width 3 ft. 6 in. Wt. 1000 lbs.

SQUARE GRAND PIANO New Style, No. 2,200 7⅓ Oct. Elegant Rosewood case, Rich Mouldings, double extra wrest plank, Carved Legs and Lyre, **All Round Corners**, French Grand Action, Best Iron Frame, all improvements complete, with stool, book and cover, only............... **$222.75**

Write for Catalogue.

☞ **Address or call upon DANIEL F. BEATTY, Washington, New Jersey.**

MUS27-03

MUS27-02

MUS27-04

MUS27-05

MUS27-06

MUS27-01

92 ADVERTISEMENTS.

BEATTY'S BEETHOVEN GRAND ORGANS

NEW STYLE, No. 9000.

The beauty of this, my newest and most perfect style, is something phenomenal. THIS MATCHLESS INSTRUMENT is without a peer, and is undoubtedly the finest organ yet manufactured. In its marvelous stop work it stands unapproached and for refined and beautiful tone qualities it can have no rival.

THE BEETHOVEN GRAND ORGAN has five (5) Octaves, 14 OCTAVES of Golden Tongue reeds and twenty-seven (27) Stops as described in the specification of stop work below. New effects are introduced which are unequaled. The case is an architectural design of rare beauty and is simply incomparable at the price. It is of solid walnut with extra large ornamental designs in fret work and carving; receptacle for music and book rack; music holder of chaste design; carved handles for moving, panelled sliding fall with lock; two turned lamp stands; metal foot plates which never wear out; best rubber upright bellows; the whole being charmingly decorated with arabesque designs in gold. Words are inadequate to convey a just conception of its surprising qualities. Height, 75 inches; Length, 46 inches; Depth, 24 inches; Weight boxed, 400 pounds.

Sent on One Month's Test Trial

27 Matchless Stops.

ONLY $60

STOP SPECIFICATIONS

1. Cello, 8 ft. tone.
2. Melodia, 8 ft. tone.
3. Clarabella, 8 ft. tone.
4. Manual Sub-Bass, 16 ft.
5. Bourdon, 16 ft. tone.
6. Saxaphone, 8 ft. tone.
7. Viol di Gamba, 8 ft. tone.
8. Diapason, 8 ft. tone.
9. Viola Dolce, 4 ft. tone.
10. Grand Expressione.
11. French Horn, 8 ft. tone.
12. Harp Æolienne.
13. Vox Humana.
14. Echo, 8 ft. tone.
15. Dulciana, 8 ft. tone.
16. Clarionet, 8 ft. tone.
17. Voix Celeste, 8 ft. tone.
18. Violina, 4 ft. tone.
19. Vox Jubilante, 8 ft.
20. Piccalo, 4 ft. tone.
21. Coupler Harmonique.
22. Orchestral Forte.
23. Grand Organ Knee Stop.
24. Right Organ Knee Stop
25. Automatic Valve Stop.
26. Right Duplex Damper.
27. Left Duplex Damper.

Beatty's Patent Stop Action,

by which TONE MODULATION is placed within the reach of the amateur as well as the professional. No other make has this great improvement.

THIS INCOMPARABLE ORGAN is entirely new in design and detail. The 14 Octaves of Reeds are arranged upon a new plan by which lovely combinations may be produced. SPECIAL ATTENTION IS CALLED TO THE NEW DUPLEX DAMPERS and

PICCALO AND SAXAPHONE

Solo Stops. Order and test at home and you will be surprised and delighted.

REMEMBER It is guaranteed 6 years and warranted as represented. Do not order an Organ until you have seen this or SEND FOR FULL description of this and many beautiful styles.

REMIT by Money Order, Express Prepaid, Bank Draft, or Registered Letters. Money refunded and all freight charges paid if not as represented.

Come to Washington, New Jersey, and see Factory (3 acres of space within walls of building) and select in person ... carriage for ... all trains.

☞ Order direct from this Advertisement, nothing saved by long correspon... do not want an Organ yourself please hand or mail this office to some ...

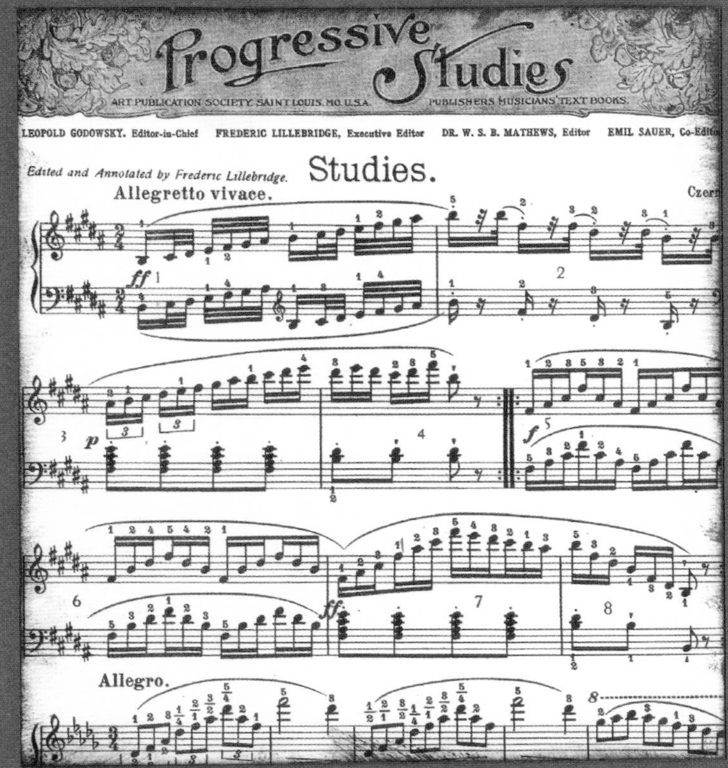

ADVERTISEMENTS.

STEY

Every buyer should
Select an Organ
That guarantees good
Every day work and
Years of service.

Every Estey Organ
Sold is made
Throughout with
Equal fidelity, and
Yields unrivaled tones.

RGAN

Send for Illustrated Catalogue. J. ESTEY & CO., Brattleboro, Vt.

MUS28-03

MUS28-02

MUS28-06

MUS28-04

MUS28-05

MUS28-01

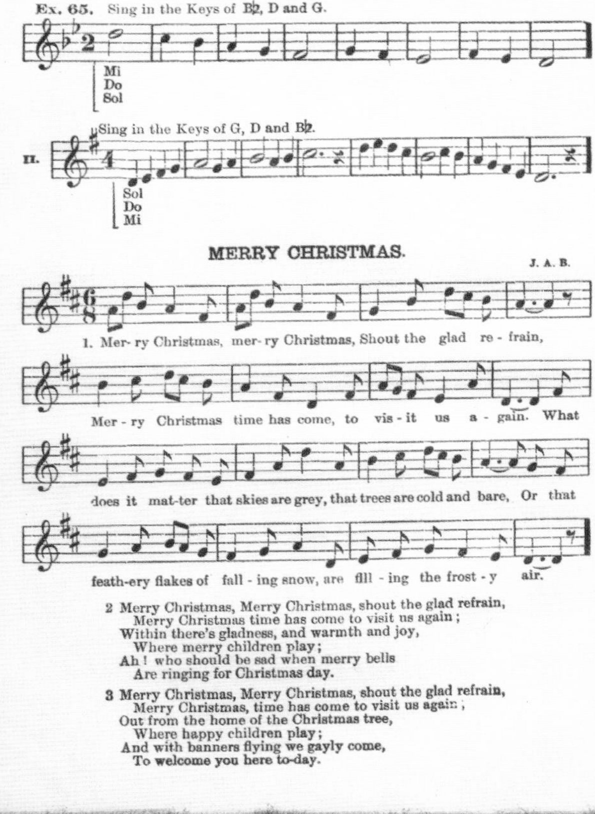
52

THREE KEY EXERCISE.

Ex. 65. Sing in the Keys of B♭, D and G.

Mi
Do
Sol

Sing in the Keys of G, D and B♭.

II.

Sol
Do
Mi

MERRY CHRISTMAS.

J. A. B.

1. Mer-ry Christmas, mer-ry Christmas, Shout the glad re-frain,
Mer-ry Christmas time has come, to vis-it us a-gain. What
does it mat-ter that skies are grey, that trees are cold and bare, Or that
feath-ery flakes of fall-ing snow, are fill-ing the frost-y air.

2 Merry Christmas, Merry Christmas, shout the glad refrain,
Merry Christmas time has come to visit us again;
Within there's gladness, and warmth and joy,
Where merry children play;
Ah! who should be sad when merry bells
Are ringing for Christmas day.

3 Merry Christmas, Merry Christmas, shout the glad refrain,
Merry Christmas, time has come to visit us again;
Out from the home of the Christmas tree,
Where happy children play;
And with banners flying we gayly come,
To welcome you here to-day.

MUS29-03

MUS29-02

MUS29-06

MUS29-04

MUS29-05

MUS29-01

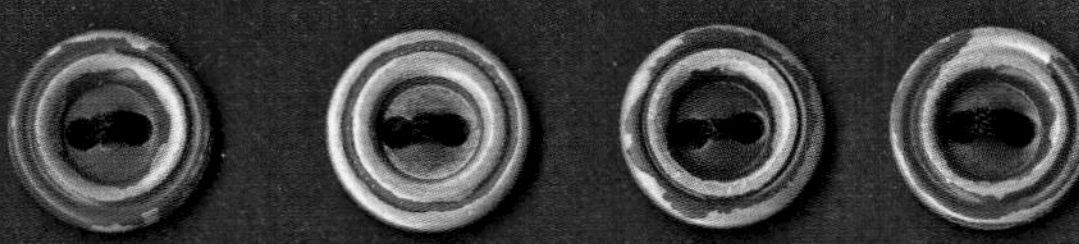

100
SPRINGTIME.
1. Now laughing with sun-light the heavens are blue, The fields
2. We roam thro' the woods where the dogwood is white, Where vio-
flow - ers are springing a - new, With leaves and white blos-so
Spring beau- ties glad- den the sight; All na - ture is beam-i
or-chard grows fair, And birds with sweet mu-sic are fill - ing the
glad-ness and love, With trees all in blos-som and blue skies a -

Stella
Sweetest in Tone.
STELLA
Best in Quality.
A music box with a
PIANO TONE
Playing any number of tunes, with smooth metallic tune sheets. No pins or projections to break off. Write for catalogue.
JACOT & SON 39 Union Sq., New York.
Department C

MUSIC
66

NO MORE WELCOME PRESENT CAN BE FOUND THAN A
REGINA MUSIC BOX
(On exhibition and for sale at all first-class music stores.)
THE REGINA is not a toy, but a marvelous instrument, rendering the most difficult music with exquisite sweetness and expression. PLAYS 1,000 TUNES; classic, popular and sacred. Has a strong, massive movement, and, unlike other music boxes, does not get out of order. Prices from $7 to $70. Send for Free Descriptive Catalogue telling about the most wonderful music box ever made.
THE NEW ORCHESTRAL REGINA, the largest of all music boxes, is described in a separate circular that will interest proprietors of Hotels, Winter Resorts and other public places. Tells how to make

503
LOVE'S OLD SWEET SONG
J.L. MOLLOY
MICHAEL BANNER
dante con moto
Sul D
pp semplice
rit.
a tempo
pp
III Corde
rit.
espressivo

MUS30-03

MUS30-02

MUS30-06

MUS30-04

MUS30-05

MUS30-01

The first requisite in a Player-piano is a real piano.
That's the Emerson Piano.
The second requisite is a player mechanism that has the "human" quality of "human" expression.
That's the Emerson Player-Piano.
Each is assured by the Emerson quality.
Both are secured in the Emerson Player-Piano.

Illustrated catalogue free.

Dealers in Principal Cities and Towns.

EMERSON PIANO CO.
BOSTON, MASS.

MINARY STEPS. 15

5 6 7 8 9
10 11 12 13
14 15 16 17
18 19 20
21 22 23

lesson. This will be suggested to her by the chart exercise. For instance, if the chart exercise is a study of *Sol*, Sol may become the center of interest in the dictation exercise, and by following in a general way the exercise on the chart she will establish the point. She should, however, not be guided by the position given to Sol in the chart exercise, but should

Department for Children

Edited by Miss Jo-Shipley Watson

[The Etude takes pleasure in presenting a portrait of the genial and practical editor of the Children's Department, Miss Jo-Shipley Watson. Miss Watson has had a most thorough training for her work, and is now a highly successful teacher in the Middle West. After spending two years at Wellesley College under Junius W. Hill (a remarkably fine pedagog), Miss Watson went to Europe, where she remained, studying music for three years under Martin Krause in Leipsic and Heinrich Barth at the Hochschule in Berlin. Later she had additional courses in special work in America under Edward MacDowell, Alfred Ross Parsons and Carl Faelton. She has taught in Emporia, Kansas, and in Kansas City. Our readers are familiar with the stimulating freshness, practical usefulness and wholesome optimism which makes her department in The Etude so near to the child soul and so helpful to those who work with children.—Editor of The Etude.]

Mary (*looking up*): We couldn't even know enough to put two pieces of wood together, much less play our own pieces.

Haydn (*turning to Mary*): You modern children have so much done for you—you scarcely need to invent amusements—why I do believe that your teachers do most of your thinking for you—very bad, very bad! My first teacher gave me real discipline, and I received more beating than bread or instruction; my second one was no better, he punished and scolded like a tyrant.

Mary (*excitedly*): Oh Herr Haydn—did he ever rap your knuckles?

blew so much that I c
taper lighted. I acco
deal of reading here, a
went to my second garr
fortune to have an inf
I also had a clavier.
poet Metastasio, introd
pora, the famous teach

Ben (*inquiringly*):
one for whom you
blacked boots?

Haydn (*laughing*):
pora, I doubt if he wo
day had I not done t
for him. He was no
either, but I had sple
of meeting famous pe
and my good fortune s
Porpora's garret. I pr
orized six sonatas of E
great Bach's son. I ow
Emanuel Bach. His *T*
Playing was most val
learned the habit of
It was while I was at
gave my first lessons, f
sum of two dollars a
month.

Ben *and* Mary (*in c*

MUS31-03

MUS31-02

MUS31-06

MUS31-04

MUS31-05

MUS31-01

Sleep and Dream
M. M. ♩ = 60
Sleep and dream dar - ling, moth - er is nigh. An - gels are
la - bye. Fold - ed the ti - ny hands dim - pled
are the blue eyes mer - ry and bright.
pp
(Baby's asleep and

MUS32-02

MUS32-06

MUS32-07

MUS32-03

MUS32-04

MUS32-05

MUS32-01

A Madeleine Baron
LA PETITE DUCHESSE
Gavotte Louis XV
By HENRI BARON
Allegretto
Piano
In The Valley Of Roses With You
Andantino.
VIOLIN and PIANO.
CARL VOGT.
Boat Song.
Moderato.
CARL VOGT.
Remembrance.
Moderato.
Lest we Forget
BLUE BIRDS
HESITATION WALTZ
stars come out

MUS33-02

MUS33-04

MUS33-03

MUS33-08

MUS33-07

MUS33-05

MUS33-06

MUS33-01

107
The Birthday
Words by
OLYN S. BAILEY
Music by
MARY B. EHRMANN
Semplice
I am six years old. It's my birth - day. When I
I shall have a cake with thick frost - ing. Sev - en
stand by the knob of the door, You can see I'm a lit - tle bit
can - dles on top I shall see, And be - cause I am tall - er and
tall - er,
old - er,

MUS34-03

MUS34-02

MUS34-06

MUS34-04

MUS34-05

MUS34-01

In Slumber Sweet
Revised and fingered by
THOS. a'BECKET.
Moderato.
PIANO
p innocente.
Presented by
Aaron Garber,
New Buena Vista.
Presented By

MUS35-04

MUS35-03

MUS35-02

MUS35-07

MUS35-06

MUS35-05

MUS35-01

THE ETUDE
SWEET MEMORIES
Andante
Moderato
GEORGE DUDLEY MARTIN
HAPPY DAYS OF CHILDHOOD

MUS36-03

MUS36-02

MUS36-04

MUS36-05

MUS36-06

MUS36-01

INSTITUTE OF MUSICAL ART

OF THE CITY OF NEW YORK

53 Fifth Avenue, New York — FRANK DAMROSCH, Director

Established and endowed for the education of serious students of music. Offers all advantages of a European musical education. Faculty composed of the most eminent teachers of Europe and America.

Prospectus on application to the Registrar.

A HOLIDAY SUGGESTION

A PLEASING GIFT FOR THE MUSIC LOVER

Title Cover December 1905 in 8 Colors

A PERPETUAL REMINDER OF YOUR LOVING THOUGHTFULNESS

A Subscription for "THE ETUDE"

¶ THE CHRISTMAS NUMBER and a beautiful HOLIDAY CARD bearing your name will be mailed to your friend to arrive on Christmas Morning. The Subscription will also be entered for the year 1906—13 issues.

¶ SPECIAL OFFERS.—Write us to-day for a special premium

cently, the ... regarding it as on the whole better, safer, and quite as easy in the long run, to *employ strict fingering in every instance.* The fourth ...hich in some of the black key positions is re- ...t first, presently reconciles itself to the some-

the proper fingering to be impracticable for the individual player.

The three positions are shown below, as they appe for both hands, with the proper fingering.

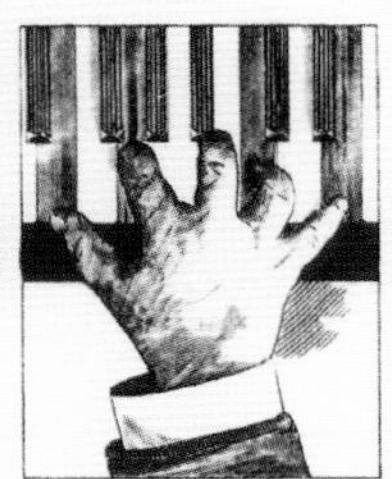

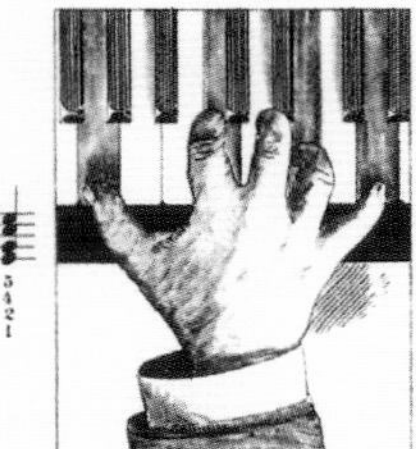

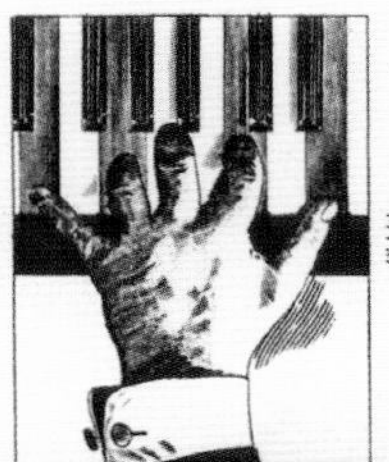

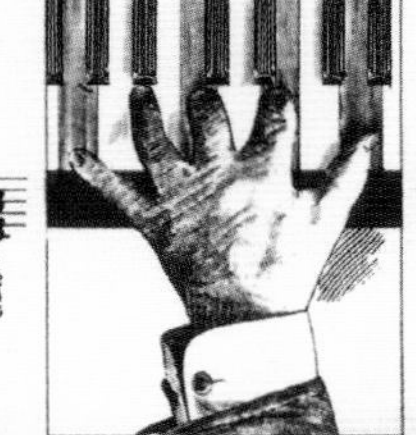

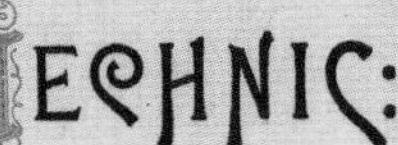

Touch and Technic:

FOR

Artistic • Piano • Playing.

BY MEANS OF A NEW COMBINATION OF EXERCISE-FORMS AND METHOD OF PRACTICE, CONDUCTING RAPIDLY TO EQUALITY OF FINGER POWER, FACILITY AND EXPRESSIVE QUALITY OF TONE.

BY

DR. WILLIAM MASON.

MUS37-04

MUS37-03

MUS37-02

MUS37-07

MUS37-05

MUS37-06

MUS37-01

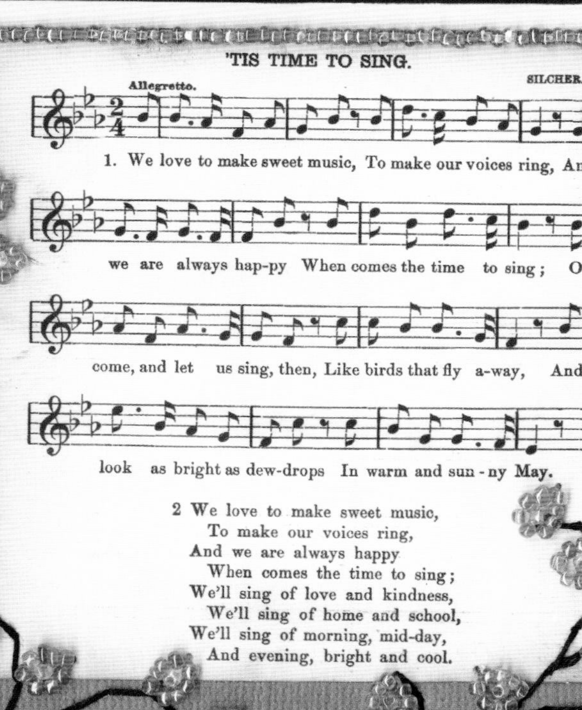

'TIS TIME TO SING.

Allegretto. SILCHER.

1. We love to make sweet music, To make our voices ring, And we are always hap-py When comes the time to sing; O come, and let us sing, then, Like birds that fly a-way, And look as bright as dew-drops In warm and sun-ny May.

2 We love to make sweet music,
To make our voices ring,
And we are always happy
When comes the time to sing;
We'll sing of love and kindness,
We'll sing of home and school,
We'll sing of morning, mid-day,
And evening, bright and cool.

MUS38-02

MUS38-03

MUS38-04

MUS38-01

The Little Drummer
5
Mar-cia M. M. ♩ = 120
3
(The drums coming nearer)
Rub, dub
March-ing to the drum sing
rub, dub, dub,
March-ing to the drum sing
rub, dub, dub.
Rub, dub
ppp

MUS39-03

MUS39-02

MUS39-06

MUS39-04

MUS39-05

MUS39-01

21
With Drums and Colors Flying.
MARCH.
Revised and Fingered by
A. BECHTER.
RICHARD EILENBERG, Op. 210. Nº 1.
Allegretto.
PIANO.
(A)

MUS40-03

MUS40-02

MUS40-05

MUS40-04

A·BOOK OF UNIQUE CHILDREN'S SONGS

For the HOME—SCHOOL—KINDERGARTEN

MERRY SONGS FOR LITTLE FOLKS

Words by WM. H. GARDNER Illustrations by JEROME P. UHL Music by LOUIS F. GOTTSCHALK

Including Actions and Tableaux. Price, $1.50

THE most elaborate work ever issued by this house. The illustrations are by an artist of national reputation. Every page is illumined in three colors, the work of perhaps the finest art printers in America.

The authors as well as the illustrator are ardent lovers of children. Every verse, every melody, every illustration is bright, original, and attractive; the humor is by turns quaint, nonsensical, and attractive. The work is considered by all who have examined it to be the superior of any book of Children's Songs yet on the market.

The songs are in the style of nonsense verses with catchy rhythms and jingling rhymes. The music is melodious and aptly fits the words, not at all difficult, and within the compass of the child voice. The piano accompaniments are effective and characteristic.

Numerous directions are given for the use of the various numbers as Action Songs, and for the arrangement of appropriate Tableaux.

There are in the book 22 songs suitable for all the various purposes to which a book of Children's Songs could be put. For the home and school the songs can be sung with or without actions or tableaux; for kindergarten or exhibition purposes the actions or tableaux or both, may be carried out most effectively.

THEO. PRESSER, 1712 Chestnut Street, Philadelphia

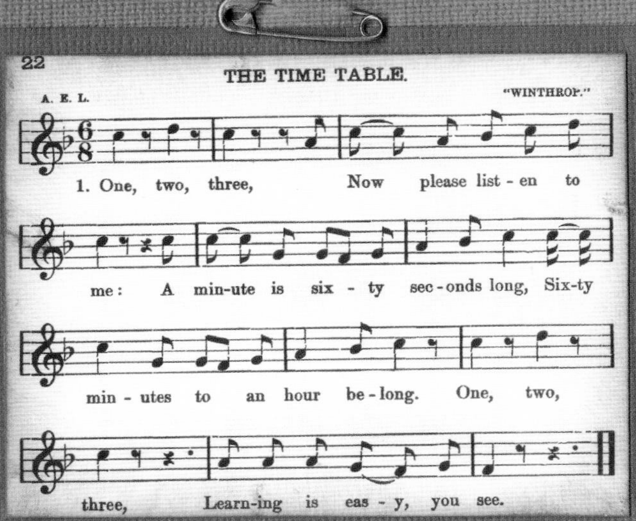

22
THE TIME TABLE.
A. E. L.
"WINTHROP."
1. One, two, three, Now please list - en to
me: A min-ute is six - ty sec-onds long, Six-ty
min - utes to an hour be - long. One, two,
three, Learn-ing is eas - y, you see.

MUS41-03

MUS41-02

MUS41-04

MUS41-05

MUS41-01

A BIRD OF PARADISE.
AN INTERMEZZO
BY JASON V. MATHEWS.
A Bird of Paradise.
Intermezzo.
Allegretto grazioso.
JASON V. MATHEWS.
quasi pizz.

MUS42-03

MUS42-02

MUS42-04

MUS42-05

MUS42-06

MUS42-07

MUS42-01

LITTLE LORD FAUNTLEROY

WALTZES

Respectfully dedicated to Master Wallie Eddinger

BY

[Henny] Boeckner.

6

Baltimore

Geo. Willig & Co

442

THE ETUDE

Bac… …e laid aside, as the studies may be, afte… …acticing. A student who had spent wee… …the "English Suites," and flattered him… …st it was satisfactory, was surprised to … …e end of the lesson: "Good; *now lear*…

Stri… …is pupils soon learn to delight in …se which at first seems to them the …t praise of condemnation. For he is s… …f. "Music is too sacred a thing to mak… …s about." And he is as severe with him… …with his pupils. They may be thankful … That has been practiced as I wished it; … …cky indeed to have as a rare commen… …rd that played so, I should say an arti… …" and to be told: "I would be will… …szt hear you play his concerto," that is t… …, and happens to few!

Int… thr… Poi… In studying the greater compositions, one is struck with the individuality which is brought out for each composer. And it is a somewhat dazzling sensation, eve… …t proficient, after weeks, or months, per… …ver points which at times seem discou… …rous and painfully fine, to feel in a fi… …have *the thing* that is meant. It is you… …and to reproduce. And then you rea… …pretation can never be a matter of boo… …, polishing, hearing, repeating—from ear… …om finger to finger is the tradition. An… …is for your later, independent study. As a young student, Baermann had

MEN AND THINGS OF THE DAY IN MUSIC.

BY ARTHUR ELSON.

THE operatic ventures of Richard Strauss have not proved successful, yet the advent of his new "Salome," soon to be given at Dresden, promises to be an important event. The libretto is based on the work of Oscar Wilde, and the score gains interest from the presence of a new instrument, the Heckelphone. This addition to the orchestra is not a "freak," like the famous wind machine, but a new member of the oboe family, made by Heckel at Biebrich. It is keyed like the oboe, but gives a tone that is fuller and richer, stronger even than that of the English horn.

Speaking of new instruments, the Ritter quartet is still causing discussion. It consists of violin, Ritter viola, tenor violin (an octave below the usual tuning), and bass violin, larger than the 'cello. While its effects are highly interesting, present opinion rates it as a new combination rather than a substitute for the classical string quartet.

New operas are the rule abroad. Siegfried Wagner's fourth venture, "Bruder Lustig," is billed for November 11th, at Hamburg. Like his other works, it has a legendary subject, this time drawn from an Austrian source. Humperdinck is at work on "Das Wunder von Köln," while his "Heirat Wider Willen" has reached the Italian theatres. Max Vogrich, whose "Buddha" aroused interest recently, is bringing out

The music… was handicapped by a poor li… play piece, given at Nîmes, was "… by Xavier Leroux. That compo… Fiamette" won such renown, "Chemineau," and is now at … Paul Vidal is attacking an Eg… "Rameses."

Italy, too, furnishes her quo… Mascagni's "Amica," treating a S… is just now holding the public at… accustomed to seeing new Masc… sudden eclipse. Leoncavallo, und… on his "Roland of Berlin," is pl… comedy, entitled, "The Youth of… said to have gone to Spain in "… Franchetti's "Figlia di Jorio" is… Scala Theatre, in Milan. His wor… in America, but many of his… most exaggerated praise to his m…

The national talent of Belgiu… evidence at the recent royal fe… "Patriotic March" was earnest to … nity, while Tinel's "Te Deum" also … of the occasion. Jan Blockx … galm," or Flemish festal hymn, … "Princesse de l'Auberge" and "F… were given at the theatres.

In England, the period of autumn leaves and … sical festivals has come. Dvorák once remarke…

MUS43-03

MUS43-02

MUS43-04

MUS43-07

MUS43-05

MUS43-06

MUS43-01

"Used by all Up-to-Date Teachers"
THE KINDER
Adjustable Foot Rest
and
Pedal Extenders for the Piano
The children who use them learn twice as fast and practice twice as much with half the exertion.
Foot Rest $3.00. Pedal Extenders $2.00 per set of two.
Special discount to teachers and trade. Sold by all first class music houses. Agents wanted.
Illustrated catalog for the asking.
W. MARKS, 145 West Eighty-Fourth Street, NEW YORK
Brilliant Piano Music for Social and Recital Use
MODERN DRAWING ROOM PIECES
For the Piano. PRICE $1.00.
Contains exclusively brilliant and attractive drawing-room compositions of a high order, melodious and showy in the hands of the average player. Modern pieces of striking character and proven popularity, every one sure to be appreciated by the general musical listener.
No further suggestion as to the high value of this work is needed than a mention of a few of the composers represented: Borowski, Paul Wachs, MacDowell, Reinecke and Kölling.
1712 Chestnut St., Philadelphia, Pa
THE MUSIC OF EXISTENCE.
EACH one of us may make life a strain of music if we will. If our lives are humdrum we can live them with the immortal simplicity of a folk-song, which impresses the commonplaces of existence with the beauty of sorrow, hope or joy, and brings comfort to souls untouched by great symphonies. These symphonies, too—amid their magnificent complexities of interwoven interests we must remember the foundation theme that makes them purpose beautiful. The pioneer and the wande wild Hamelin music that beckons roads of the world. Some liv the sympathetic ear can fi and minuet the note of
FRIENDSHIP SONGS
By Tod B. Galloway
PRICE, $1.25
A set of seven vocal gems similar to the well-known "MEMORY SONGS" by the same writer.
"HUSHABY BABY," "ALONE," "HEAVEN," "DESIRE," "FOUR-LEAFED CLOVER,"
1712 Chestnut St., PHILA., Pa.
TRUE MUSICAL UNDERSTANDING. IS IT THE RESULT OF RULE AND MEASURE?
BY ARMANDE DE POLIGNAC.
[From the French by Florence Leonard.]
ALAS, that so many persons have pianos! Numberless others devote themselves to studying some instrument, and these, when they can perform upon the elephant's tusk or the catgut, offend us either by their ignorance or their too complete knowledge. They learn a few rules, apply them anywhere and everywhere; we suffer from hearing Beethoven rhythms crowded into two-bar effects, instead of spreading out in larger groups; we hear dynami treated with absolute ignorance, or rather absol lack of curiosity concerning this side of form; hear arbitrary interpretations of the various s which mean staccato, portamento and so on. In ng a fugue, these zealots forget that here is co ubject, or they exclaim if they hear a ca imple imitation: "Ah, there is a fugue!" who would gladly list
The laity of art, erstand, or for the love
12
PRELIMINARY STEPS.
7 8 9 10 11 12 13
13. In these exercises it will be noticed that the succession at first is long, including the entire scale, and that it continues in one direction to the end; that as the exercises progress they become shorter and also progress down and up or up and down in the same example. This illustrates the line of development, and shows that the advancement is in the line of fewer and fewer tones until a succession of only two tones is heard — this being the point of greatest difficulty. When the children readily distinguish between Do, Re and Do, Ti, the work is well advanced.
Oral Dictation.
14. Having established the power to discriminate between descending and ascending successions, the teacher extends the child's power to hear and to discriminate till he can tell not only in what direction the succession progresses, but what the tones used are. That is, after the teacher has
Loo, or loo.
en to sing the same exercise, of the scale have been well g Do, Ti; or Do, Re. ifficulty of this exercise, used. In the beginning, tablish clearly that the e exercises containing the entire course, and is
Hahn Violin School
FREDERICK E. HAHN, Director
1524 Chestnut Street, Philadelphia, Pa.
RICK MAXSON Organist First Baptist Church Philadelphia
Teacher of Organ, Piano and Theory
FIRST BAPTIST CHURCH PHILADELPHIA
STUDIO OF MUSIC
Miss Helen Esther Wilkinson
Former pupil of PROF. OSCAR RAIF, Berlin.
Present pupil of MAITRE ISADORE PHILIPP, Paris.
(Please send for Catalogue.)
5948 Germantown Ave., Germantown, Pa.
HUGH A. CLARKE MUS. DOC.
223 South 38th Street Philadelphia
LESSONS BY MAIL IN HARMONY, COUNTERPOINT AND COMPOSITION
INCORPORATED 1900
THE PENNSYLVANIA
COLLEGE OF MUSIC
DEGREES OF MUSIC CONFERRED
K. H. CHANDLER, PREST.
1511 GIRARD AVE.
UNIVERSITY SCHOOL of MUSIC
ANN ARBOR, MICHIGAN
Twenty-five Members
BUSH TEMPLE CONSERVATORY
NORTH CLARK STREET AND CHICAGO AVENUE, CHICAGO
KENNETH M. BRADLEY, Director.
BOARD OF EXAMINERS
MUSIC ORATORY AND LANGUAGES
Sherwood Music S
WM. H. SHERWOOD, Director
M. H. SHERWO
Concerts and Lecture R
MISS L. HUMPHREY
713 Fine Arts Building, Chicago
GOOD MUSIC LIVES FOREVER
Back Numbers of "1904" and "1905"
THE ETUDE
The reading matter as good to-day as the day of issue.
We have these issues done up in bundles at
25 CENTS PER BUNDLE.
More than 30 Pieces of Music in each Package.
Address THE ETUDE, 1712 Chestnut Street, Philadelphia, Pa.

MUS44-03

MUS44-02

MUS44-04

MUS44-05

MUS44-09

MUS44-08

MUS44-10

MUS44-06

MUS44-07

MUS44-01

MOTHER GOOSE
SET TO MUSIC
MELODIES.
McLOUGHLIN BROS. NEW YORK
Child's Play.
(Tändelei.)
FRANCOIS BEHR, Op. 575. Nº 3.
Allegretto scherzando.
PIANO.
NATURAL MUSIC COURSE
HARMONIC PRIMER
FREDERIC H. RIPLEY & THOMAS TAPPER
AMERICAN · BOOK · COMPANY
NEW YORK · CINCINNATI · CHICAGO
6

MUS45-03

MUS45-02

MUS45-06

MUS45-04

MUS45-05

MUS45-01

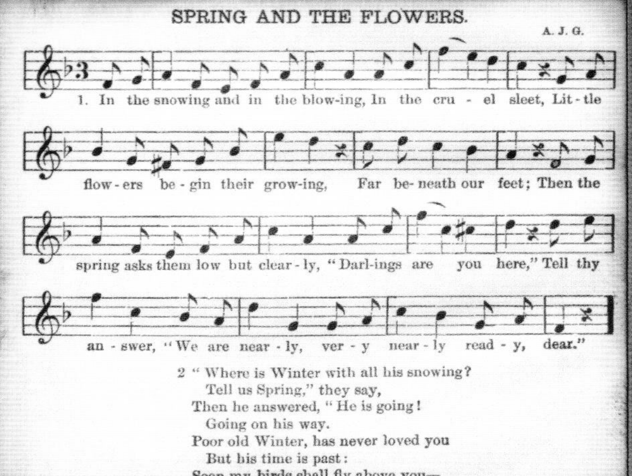
SPRING AND THE FLOWERS.

A. J. G.

1. In the snowing and in the blow-ing, In the cru - el sleet, Lit - tle flow - ers be - gin their grow-ing, Far be-neath our feet; Then the spring asks them low but clear-ly, "Darl-ings are you here," Tell thy an - swer, "We are near - ly, ver - y near - ly read - y, dear."

2 "Where is Winter with all his snowing?
Tell us Spring," they say,
Then he answered, "He is going!
Going on his way.
Poor old Winter, has never loved you
But his time is past:
Soon my birds shall fly above you—
They will set you free at last."

LESSON 19.

TWO PART SINGING.

45. When each of two voices sings a different *melody* or **PART** at the same time, we then called it **TWO PART SINGING.**

NOTE. In exercise 80, and all others which are marked *Reversible Ex.*, **ALL** the voices should sing the music and words on the two staffs beginning with the *upper*; then all the voices should begin with the *lower* staff and end with the *upper*. For *two part singing* half of the voices begin with the *upper staff* and the other half with the *lower staff*. Thus the music on the upper and lower staff is sung at the same time, both parts singing the same words.

Ex. 80. One and Two Part Reversible Ex.

A cheer for the snow the drift ing snow,
Much whit - er and pur - er than all things be - low.

46. When two different *melodies* or *parts* are printed on the same staff, the stems of the notes of the *upper part* will be turned up, and the stems of the notes of the *lower part*, will be turned down. When one part is silent the *rest* is placed above or below the other part.

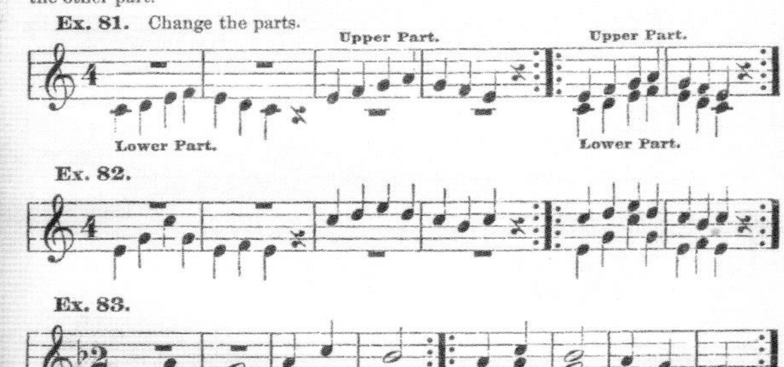
Ex. 81. Change the parts.

Upper Part.
Upper Part.
Lower Part.
Lower Part.

Ex. 82.

Ex. 83.

MUS46-03

MUS46-02

MUS46-04

MUS46-05

MUS46-06

MUS46-01

THE ETUDE
CRADLE SONG
WIEGENLIED
JOH. BRAHMS
1. Lul - la - by and good night, with
1. Gu - ten A - bend, gut' Nacht, mit
2. Lul - la - by and good night, thy
2. Gu - ten A - bend, gut' Nacht, von
ro - ses be - dight, with li - lies be - sted is ba - by's wee
Ro - sen be - dacht, mit Näg - lein be - steckt schlüpf' un - ter die
mo - ther's de - light, bright an - gels a - round
Eng - lein be - wacht, die zei - gen im Traum

TEACHERS!! TEACHERS!!

SCHOOLS, CONVENTS, AND CONSERVATORIES OF

MUSIC

ARE SUPPLIED WITH EVERYTHING NEEDED IN THEIR WORK

PROMPTLY — ECONOMICALLY — SATISFACTORILY

By THEO. PRESSER, PHILADELPHIA, PA.

The unique but reasonable methods of the music supply house of THEO. PRESSER, the outgrowth of his intimate knowledge as a teacher of their needs, and perfected during twenty years as a publisher, have revolutionized the music-dealing trade.

It will pay every one interested in any manner to investigate at first hand the liberal system and policy followed by this house in its efforts to—

Publish Modern Teaching Material;
To Give the Best Discounts Possible in Every Case;
To Allow the Most Satisfactory Terms;
To Carry a Stock (no matter where published, or by whom) that will Contain Everything of Value to Music Teachers and Students; and
Thus to Aid the Cause of Musical Education and lighten the labors of its followers.

In the new building, 1712-1714 Chestnut Street, Philadelphia, Pa., lately purchased and remodeled for the best use of this business, with its six floors carefully planned and stocked with everything needed in the Music Teacher's work, we cannot say too strongly that we are

Equipped to Supply Every Teacher and School of Music in this Country and Canada

No matter how small or how large the trade, with everything needed.

THE ON SALE PLAN (original with us) is arranged and carried out on a far more liberal basis than obtainable from any of our imitators. We will gladly allow any teacher the use and advantages derived from this plan, and the same liberal discounts, even if they desire to place their regular orders elsewhere.

All Orders, Large or Sma...
All Orders are Attended to...

ized parts there is a chance for all who possess ability, average intelligence and plain every honesty.—*Musical Courier.*

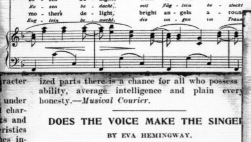

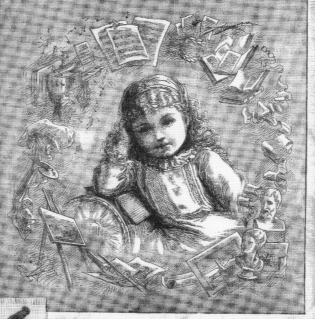

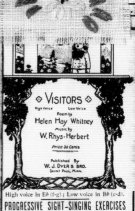

DOES THE VOICE MAKE THE SINGE[R]

BY EVA HEMINGWAY.

EMERSON says: "We are all wise. The diffe[rence] between persons is not in wisdom but in art." E[very] person has something of a voice and some insight [into] the gift of song, but not to every one with a voice [does] nature grant the power of song.

Voice does not make the singer, but with [it] must be united intellect (constructive intellect), [that] is, an intellect that can concentrate intense pa[...] around a single subject, can discriminate upon [...] to intensify. Philosopher Bain says: "Mind s[...] from discrimination." With such an intellect wi[...] singer detach the best from his subject and th[...] build a satisfying structure for his phrases. He [can] also gracefully pass from one subject to an[other,] from Oratorio to the Ballad, making the one a[s ef]fective as the other.

Intellect and voice, however, are not sufficie[nt to] consummate the art of singing. Impulse, [...] wedded to intellect, brings forth tone-color, hen[ce ...] getting the dramatic and lyric t[...] ing with how much impulse o[...] best acts are spontaneous, henc[e ...] strong impulse or transient me[...] which would communicate instan[...] ence, if the singer would sway [...] tions by which he is possessed while singing. The stronger the impulse, the more effective the song. Admiral Dewey had impulse, this impulse which sweeps everything before it, and without which years might have been spent in fighting Spain. The artist who is the genius is the one with great passion underlying intellect and impulse. Passion makes one forget oneself, surprises out of propriety, giving one [...] abandonment of spirit. Cromwell says: "Man ne[ver] rises so high as when he knows not whither he [is] going."

◇ VISITORS ◇

High Voice Low Voice

Poem by Helen Hay Whitney

Music by W. Rhys-Herbert

Price 50 Cents

Published By W. J. DYER & BRO. SAINT PAUL, MINN.

High voice in E♭ (f-g); Low voice in B♭ (c-d).

PROGRESSIVE SIGHT-SINGING EXERCISES

By W. RHYS-HERBERT

A complete method, to be used as such, or in connection with any other system of Teaching.

PRICE 50c. { Special to Teachers: $3.60 per dozen; postage, 30c. additional.

RECENT SONGS—By W. Rhys-Herbert. The Wings of a Dove. Hymn, from the Welsh, by W. J. Gwylin. 40c. The Wonderful Story. Poem by Owen Morris. 60c. High voice in A♭ (e♭-a♭); medium voice in F; low voice in E♭. The Land Immortal. An adaptation of the melody "Simple Aveu." By Francis Thome. 50c. High voice in D (e-g); low voice in B♭, with violin obligato ad lib. Dearest. Poem by Walter Robarts. 50c. High voice in F (e-g); low voice in C. My Heart Hath a Song. Poem by Ethel M. Kelley. 50c. For low voice only, in B♭ (ab-eb). 'Neath Thy Casement. Poem by Walter Robarts. 50c. High voice in A♭ (e-ab); low voice in F.

Brilliant Piano Music for Social and Recital Use

MODERN DRAWING ROOM PIECES

For the Piano. PRICE $1.00.

Contains exclusively brilliant and attractive drawing-room compositions of a high order, melodious and showy in the hands of the average player. Modern pieces of striking character and proven popularity, every one sure to be appreciated by the general musical listener.

No further suggestion as to the high value of this work is needed than a mention of a few of the composers represented: Borowski, Paul Wachs, MacDowell, Reinecke and Kölling.

THEODORE PRESSER, Publisher, 1712 Chestnut St., Philadelphia, Pa.

MUS47-03

MUS47-02

MUS47-07

MUS47-04

MUS47-8

MUS47-09

MUS47-05

MUS47-06

MUS47-01

LEST WE FORGET
Jazzin' the Blues Away
Marcia moderato
Mis - ter let me tell you this is no place to
Wait un - til you hear that moan-in' groan-in' trom
Vamp
just got to beat it you can take it from me
Slip on your
Crash-ing of
G. SCHIRMER'S EDITION OF STANDARD INSTRUCTION BOOKS
E. D. WAGNER
FIRST INSTRUCTION BOOK FOR THE PIANOFORTE
A THOROUGH COURSE FOR TEACHERS AND PUPILS
PART I PART II
Pr. in Paper, $1.00 net
" " Boards, $1.25 "
COPYRIGHT, 1883, BY G. SCHIRMER
NEW YORK G. SCHIRMER
DESIGN COPYRIGHT 1899 BY G. SCHIRMER
EDWARD B. EDWARDS DES.

MUS48-03

MUS48-02

MUS48-06

MUS48-07

MUS48-04

MUS48-05

MUS48-01

MEET ME AT TWILIGHT
SONG
By
SYDNEY P. HARRIS
Chorus arranged for Male or mixed Quartette
HIGH
★MEDIUM
LOW
60
2/-Net
Published by
THE SYDNEY P. HARRIS CO.
Vol. 17
MARCH, 1917
No. 11
10¢ A COPY - $1.00 A YEAR
MY LOVE FOR THINE.
LOVE'S OLD SWEET SONG
J.L. MOLLOY
con moto
rit.
a tempo
espressivo

MUS49-04

MUS49-03

MUS49-02

MUS49-07

MUS49-05

MUS49-06

MUS49-01

Childish Glee.
Polka.
empo di Polka.

PROSPECTIVE PURCHASERS OF ESTEY PIANOS.

Where Can He Be?
dante
Where and Oh where is my lit - tle dog gone And where a
With his tail cut short and his ears cut long, O
he be?

MUS50-03

MUS50-02

MUS50-04

MUS50-05

MUS50-01

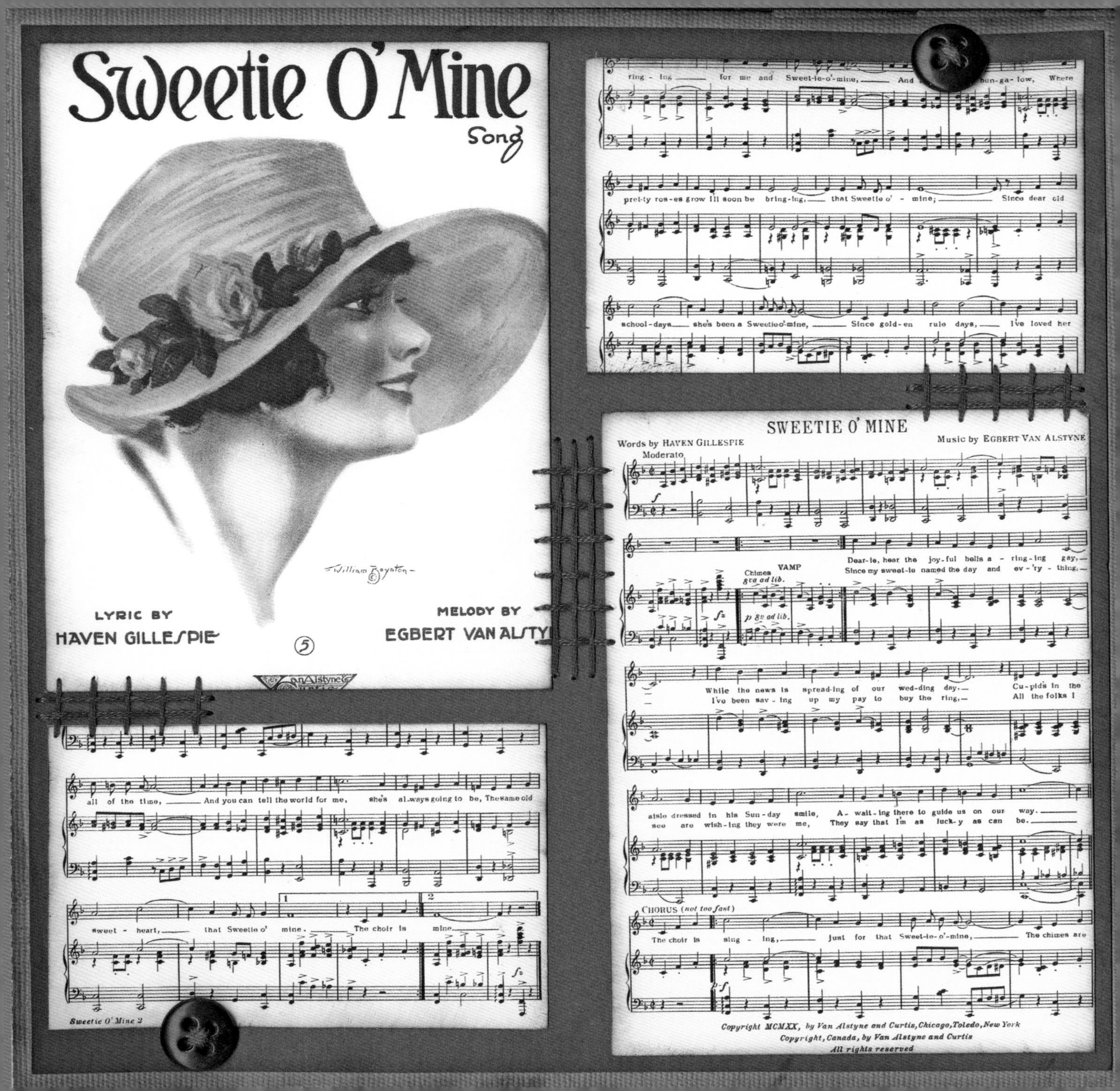

Sweetie O'Mine
Song

William Boynton

LYRIC BY
HAVEN GILLESPIE

MELODY BY
EGBERT VAN ALSTY

5

all of the time, ___ And you can tell the world for me, she's al-ways going to be, The same old
sweet - heart, ___ that Sweetie o' mine. The choir is mine.
1
2
Sweetie O' Mine 2

ring - ing ___ for me and Sweet-ie-o'-mine, ___ And ... bun-ga-low, Where
pret-ty ros-es grow I'll soon be bring-ing, ___ that Sweetie o' - mine; ___ Since dear old
school-days ___ she's been a Sweetie o'-mine, ___ Since gold-en rule days, ___ I've loved her

SWEETIE O' MINE

Words by HAVEN GILLESPIE

Music by EGBERT VAN ALSTYNE

Moderato

Chimes VAMP
8va ad lib.
p 8va ad lib.

Dear-ie, hear the joy-ful bells a - ring-ing gay, —
Since my sweet-ie named the day and ev-'ry-thing, —
While the news is spread-ing of our wed-ding day. — Cu-pid's in the
I've been sav-ing up my pay to buy the ring, — All the folks I
aisle dressed in his Sun-day smile, A-wait-ing there to guide us on our way. ___
see are wish-ing they were me, They say that I'm as luck-y as can be. ___

CHORUS (*not too fast*)

The choir is sing - ing, ___ just for that Sweet-ie-o'-mine, ___ The chimes are

MUS51-03

MUS51-02

MUS51-04

MUS51-06

MUS51-01

MUS51-05

THE ETUDE
A LITTLE SONG FOR TWO
J. EDMUND V. COOKE
TOD B. GALLOWAY
Valse moderato
A song from me to you, you say, A ten - der song for eve - ry
And were there but one theme to choose, One mo - tive ev - er - more to
day, A lit - tle song for two? Why, dear - est heart, each
use, It were noth - ing to do I'd sing all songs of
Cupid's Offerings to you

MUS52-02

MUS52-03

MUS52-04

MUS52-01

AUGUST, 1909 VOL. XXVII, No. 8

THE ETUDE

FOR THE TEACHER · STUDENT & LOVER OF MUSIC

THEO. PRESSER, PUBLISHER PHILADELPHIA, PENNA.

WHY IS A MUSICAL EDUCATION DESIRABLE?

One of our correspondents writes, "Kindly send me the five best answers that you know of to this question: 'Why should a person secure a musical education?'" Every copy of The Etude should answer this question. The advantages seem so obvious that it is very difficult to put in words all of the many reasons why one should be educated musically. However, for the benefit of our reader, and for those who may desire a similar set of reasons, we have made the following attempt. One should secure a good musical education:

1. Because the peculiar intellectual exercise and mental discipline which music affords is unexcelled.
2. Because it opens the way to one of the most delightful arts.
3. Because it is a modern means to culture demanded by society.
4. Because it affords those who practice it beneficial relaxation from their vocations.
5. Because it contributes to the joy and beauty of home life.

We might add still another reason, which, although not so pertinent to daily life, is nevertheless significant: Because music is a necessary modern mea... ressing ideas which cannot be indicated b... words, color, shape or gesture. It ... good idea for teachers to make a ... ar to the above, but evolved from ... and insert these in their circu-...

day. School books and educational magazines are now turned out by the million every week. Correspondence schools all over the world are doing a splendid work in carrying instruction to those who are so located that they can not attend a school in person. Our magazines and newspapers have long since gone outside the territory of mere news gathering, and the daily paper has become an educator. The first newspaper is said to have been published in China in 713 A. D., and it is related that even that journal, which lasted for some centuries, was in part devoted to educational problems.

In music, the art of printing has had an all-significant part. Great advances have been made within the last fifty years, and the processes have been improved and cheapened so that it is now possible to provide students with really good editions of the classics at very moderate rates. The Etude itself is really nothing more than a printed musical educator. Save for the art of printing, our readers could not obtain the information obtained in The Etu... bro... the... to t... thro... reac... Vir... day... the... a m...

waiting for the student in the little tenement room; it is standing by the teacher in the little town on the edge of the prairie; it is by the student in the small conservatory as much as the one in the greatest school of America or of Europe. Froebel, Goethe, Hugo, Walt Whitman, Mark Twain, Lincoln, Edison and Marconi never waited for opportunity. No matter in what walk of life you are, opportunity is always at hand. Just consider for one moment what the history of music might have been if Bach, Haydn, Schubert or Wagner had waited for opportunity. It is not your surroundings which will make your future. You alone are not responsible for them. You must learn to do your best amid any environment. If you form that important little habit of doing your best at all times opportunity will not be long in making your acquaintance.

A

We are told by educational specialists that the lessons which are drawn from every-

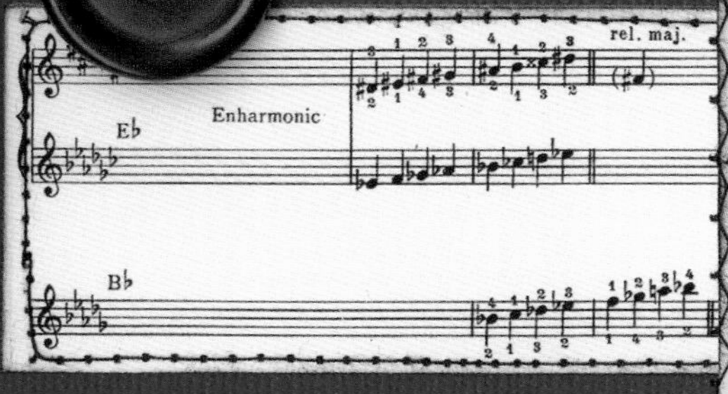

rel. maj.

E♭

Enharmonic

B♭

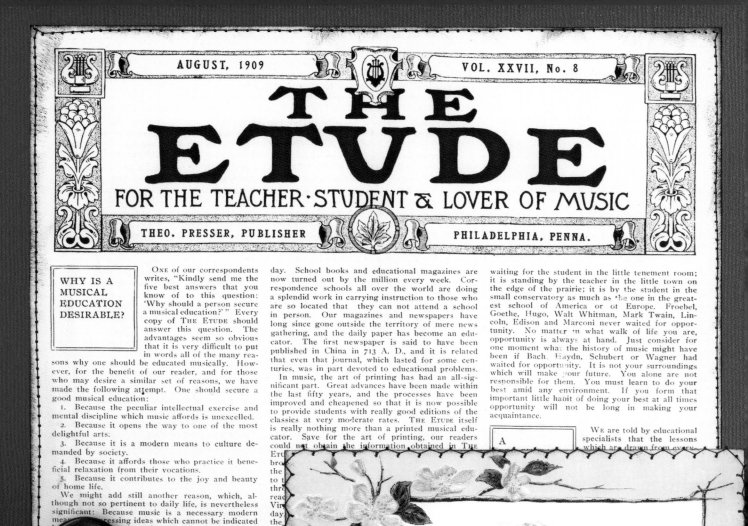

MUS53-02

MUS53-03

MUS53-05

MUS53-04

53 MUS53-01

M-O-T-H-E-R
A Word That Means The World To Me
moderato
I've been a - round the world, you bet, But nev - er went to
When I was but a ba - by, long be - fore I learned to
you bet, But nev - er went to school, Hard
be - fore I learned to walk, While
all I seem to get, Per - haps I've been a fool; But still, some ed - u - ca -
in my cra - dle, I would try my best to talk; It was - n't long,
be so swell, Would fail, if they were called up - on a sim - ple

MUS54-03

MUS54-02

MUS54-06

MUS54-04

MUS54-05

MUS54-01

VIOLIN AND PIANO
Forgotten thou wilt never be.
476
THE ETUDE
NEW YORK MUSIC SCHOOLS
You Will Hear More
Thorough, Systematic Study of
Musical Structure By
You Will Play Better
CORRESPONDENCE
For years Dr. Hanchett has taught artistic piano playing with a constant aim at true INTERPRETATION. By Hundreds of ANALYTICAL RECITALS he has revealed the vital things in the great compositions. He aims by Correspondence to show to a still larger audience what the composers mean; what there is of beauty to justify and employ hard-won technique; what may be discovered in the notes that teachers may use to truly educate, to stimulate and inspire their pupils, to appeal to their minds and hearts, to give them a real culture more lasting and valuable than the most perfect mechanism.
Subjects requiring the Teacher to HEAR the work of the student are EXCLUDED from this Course. Send for circular.
PRIVATE PIANO INSTRUCTION AT THE SCHOOL ONLY
Enjoy
MUSIC
Send for circulars and catalogues.
KATE S. CHITTENDEN, Dean of the Faculty
The Master School of Music
VOCAL DEPARTMENT
AN ENDOWED INSTITUTION IN THE INTEREST OF ART
Madame Aurelia Jaeger, Victor Beigel, Dr. Gerrit Smith, Henry T. Finck, and a full faculty of
68 West 83d St.
NEW YORK

MUS55-03

MUS55-02

MUS55-04

MUS55-05

MUS55-06

MUS55-01

Prettier Than The Prettiest
Waltz Ever Written.
Try This On Your Piano.
PRETTY LITTLE RAINBOW
Words by
ROBERT LEVENSON
Music by
VINCENT C. PLUNKETT
PIANO
'Pret-ty lit-tle Rain-bow let me see you smile a-gain, I'll kiss your

tears all a-way. Like a ray of light that's
shin-ing thro' the night, You're guid-ing me on Love's way
Revised Edition
Copyright MCMXIX by Joe Morris Music Co. 145 W. 45th St. N.Y. City.
International Copyright Secured
All Rights Reserved
FOR SALE BY ALL DEALERS!

MUS56-03

MUS56-02

MUS56-04

MUS56-05

MUS56-01

DECKER BROTHERS
MATCHLESS PIANOS
33 UNION SQUARE, N.Y.
Presented by
Aaron Garber.
DANCE OF THE VILLAGE MAIDEN
INTRO.
Allegretto con grazia M.M. ♩= 100
poco cresc.
DANCE
CHAS. LINDS
delicato
animato
Fine.

MUS57-02

MUS57-03

MUS57-06

MUS57-04

MUS57-05

MUS57-01